Praise for Harnum's book, *Basic Music Theory: How ot Read, Write, and Understand Written Music:*

"Finally someone came up with a basic music theory book that's actually understandable and readable. Mr. Harnum explains complicated concepts in a way that even someone like me without any music background can easily understand them. I am looking forward to playing an instrument thanks to his help. This is by far the best music theory book I have ever read!"

~ G. Donnald, Ellicott City, MD, USA

"The author of this book obviously had those of us who are scared of the complexity of music theory in mind when he wrote this book. Basic Music Theory is a down to earth book that moves gently through the landscape of music theory from the layout of the staff to chords and their inversions. The author also has interludes on practicing and conducting among others. I highly recommend this book if you want to understand music theory whether to compose music or to play it better."

~ Patrick Regan, Northampton, MA, USA

"*Basic Music Theory* by Jonathan Harnum, is an excellent book for people of all levels. Whether you are a beginner, or learned musician, this book is a very comprehensive source of material, that is both accessible,easy to read & understand, and very enjoyable. I have played various instruments over 24 years.And because of Harnum's matter of fact, conversational tone, this book has lent more to my understanding of basic music theory than all my private insturctors combined."

~ Remy Durant, Los Angeles, CA, USA

"Fun and engaging. A real winner!"

~ Terrie Lyons, PhD, P.C.; Portland, OR, USA

"Jonathan Harnum has taken an overly complicated subject matter and made it learable for anyone. And I do mean anyone!! As he explains early in the book, previous music theory books lack in completely explaining WHY things are the way they are. Harnum de-cryptifies all that is involved with music theory for the non-musician. But this book is not just for the non-musician! I have been a student of music for over 13 years and a teacher for 3 and I found myself finding new and interesting (and humorous) facts about music theory. This book can teach anyone music theory and keep a smile on their face the entire time."

~ Robin Giebelhausen, Chicago, IL, USA

In *Basic Music Theory: How To Read, Write, And Understand Written Music*, Jonathan Harnum draws upon more than ten years of experience and expertise as a music teacher to present the non-specialist general reader with a definitive and accessible introduction to music theory. At the end of each short chapter a review has been placed to insure that the reader has understood and assimilated the informative provided. Also provided at the conclusion of each chapter is a "practical use" exercise. At the the end of each major section or "Part" is a comprehensive review (complete with cross-referencing to the page number on which the information first appears). After every few chapters and covering other topics are "interludes" ranging from ultra-brief history of musical notation, how to practice, conducting, and a lesson in Italian musical terms. Basic Music Theory is an ideal and highly recommended text for anyone of any background wanting to become proficient in the reading, composing, and performance of written and notated music."

~ Midwest Book Review, Oregon, WI, USA

Basic Jazz Theory: volume 1

Published by Sol Ut Press
(www.sol-ut.com)

send E-mail regarding this book to BasicJazzTheory@gmail.com

ISBN 10: 1453723560
ISBN 13: 9781453723562

For general information about this book or SolUt Press, visit our web site at www.sol-ut.com.

Basic Jazz Theory
Volume 1

www.BasicJazzTheory.com

Basic Jazz Theory, vol 1
Table of Contents

THE CHAPTER EVERYONE SKIPS

The forceps of our minds are clumsy forceps, and crush the truth a little in taking hold of it.

~ H. G. Wells

In This Chapter

- Theory Isn't Everything
- Skills You'll Need
- Icons in the Book
- Overall Book Structure
- Chapter Overviews

Terms to Know

- This section will give you definitions for words in the chapter and, where there's room, jazz slang.
- book: the tunes a band plays regularly.
- clams: mistakes while playing music.
- finger zinger: someone who plays very fast.
- sitting in: to substitute or play with a group temporarily.

INTRODUCTION

Lester Young is one of the smoothest cats you'll ever hear. A jazz legend of the tenor sax, Lester Young—nicknamed *Pres* as in President—had a sweet tone and the tastiest approach to music. Check the YouTube vid of his solo on *Fine and Mellow* (http://bit.ly/nyfKt) to see and hear what I mean. Legend has it that Pres was about to take a solo and a bandmate handed him the chord changes. He waved them off, saying they messed with how he heard the music; the theory limited him in a way he didn't like. He wasn't alone. Both Bix Beiderbecke, jazz legend of the cornet, and Louis Armstrong, the jazz godfather said written notation interfered with their music. Biederbecke said he never learned how to read, but Armstrong did while in Fate Marable's band on a paddle-wheeler on the Mississippi. Pretty much all these cats could read music with ultimate fluency, but a lot of them *preferred* to use their ears because it made for better music.

The music comes first and the theory is worked out later. Step one is listen. Step two is listen some more. Step three is playing along. Then start in on the theory. Of course, in reality, it's more likely that you'll be doing all of these things at once, so my first piece of advice is that while you're trying to wrap your head around jazz theory, make sure you listen like crazy. Stuff your ears with wonder. Play along with these recordings. Later, in *Basic Jazz Theory volume 3*, I'll give you some fantastic tools to help slow down recordings to make them easier to hear and play with. For scads of links to great jazz recordings and other resources, check out www.BasicJazzTheory.com.

The other thing you should know is that *no* book will teach you how to play jazz. Books can teach you *about* things, but to actually *do* them takes something extra. Playing jazz is an art that is absorbed through intense listening, focused imitation, and fearless experimentation. The jazz masters learned on the bandstand. Literally. Another story about written music comes from the great Duke Ellington band, if memory serves. At any rate, a trumpet player was *sitting in* and when he reached for the *book*, one of his section mates said, "Oh, don't use that. We don't play it like that any more. Just listen and follow along." How would *you* do in a situation like that?

An old Zen koan says *The finger pointing at the moon is not the moon.* Jazz theory is like that. Knowing the theory behind jazz can be helpful, for sure, but it's not as helpful as listening, imitating, and emulating. Clark Terry, jazz master of the flugelhorn (a type of trumpet) said, "Imitate, assimilate, innovate."

Think of it like language. It's pretty likely that you don't know the ins and outs of semiotic theory, or what Chomsky goes on about in his generative grammar, but that doesn't interfere with your ability to speak, right? Same deal. You don't learn to spell and write until *long* after you're able to speak and be understood. Take that approach to heart with your study of jazz.

This book *will* help you understand the basics of the theory that underlies what you hear. It will also give you tools to help with the process of listening, imitating and assimilating. The innovation part is up to you. This book will help you understand things like scales, chords, progressions, standards, and a whole lot more. It's a useful book, but only one tiny piece in the jazz puzzle. It's good to remember words of wisdom from Yogi Berra: *In theory there is no difference between theory and practice, but in practice, there is.*

WHY LISTEN TO ME?

A question you're probably asking is "Why should I listen to you?," so here's my quick bio: I've been playing trumpet for over 30 years and during those decades I've also learned to play piano and guitar, as well as a smattering of percussion instruments like drum set, conga, and djembe. My current project is learning to play tabla badly (even playing tabla badly is difficult). I've been teaching music for a long time and have a few music education degrees including a Master's and am in the final stages of a PhD at Northwestern University, a leading institution in music performance, research, and teacher education. I've written a few books besides this one: *Basic Music Theory: How to Read, Write, and Understand Written Music*, and two trumpet-related books including *Sound the Trumpet: How to Blow Your Own Horn*, and *All About Trumpet*.

Improvising is where I'm at right now. I got started sitting in with bar bands in Baja improvising over pop tunes, a multitude of open mic sessions. Then I got into jazz pretty deep, and I started learning all I could on the horn and put myself into difficult and sometimes embarrassing situations in order to learn. From there I've toured with a Gypsy Jazz group and formed my own professional jazz quartet, Jazzology. I played with the top-notch Northwestern University Jazz Ensemble in the solo trumpet chair from 2005-2007, one of the most intense (and intimidating) learning experiences in improvisation I'll probably ever get. For a CD that went with my last book, *All About Trumpet*, I was lucky to play with some of the best jazz rhythm section players in Chicago, and that was a hoot! I should point out however, that they didn't play with me because they love my playing. I paid them to play with me. I'm just saying.... They're professionals of the highest caliber. I'm pretty good, but I'm not on that level, not by a long shot. I mean, these guys are monsters in the best sense of the word!

And this speaks directly to my philosophy as a teacher and musician. It's why I write these books. I'm a believer in the amateur musician, and champion of the aficionado. As Michelle Shocked says, "Music-making should not be left to the professionals." While the information in this book could lead you to fame and fortune and legendary status as a jazz icon, that is *not* why it was written. The purpose of this book is to help you understand a little more clearly some of the underpinnings of jazz theory so that you can be a better musician no matter what level you aspire to reach. This book is geared toward the comeback player, the late bloomer, the young musician, and the dabbler; it's also useful for the serious, focused student who wants to learn more. I believe that the more of us that are out there making music and sharing it with each other, the better all our lives will be. Music—jazz in particular—and musical improvisation in general are beautiful and fulfilling ways to connect with others.

SKILLS YOU'LL NEED TO MAKE THIS BOOK WORK

You'll need a basic understanding of written music to get the most out of this book, especially note names and other basic music-reading skills like sharps and flats, key signatures, rhythms, meters, and all that easy stuff. I will present information in both bass and treble clef, so if you read either one of those, you're all set. The bonus is that this is a good chance to get better at reading a clef you're unfamiliar with. For basic note-reading skills and other important information, check out another book of mine, *Basic Music Theory: How to Read, Write, and Understand Written Music*. You can get the whole thing for free online at www.sol-ut.com.

You'll need an instrument, of course, and if your instrument isn't piano, a piano will help a *lot*. It doesn't have to be a 12 foot grand piano either. A cheap electronic keyboard will do the trick. If you play guitar, that will also work. Other options are computer programs that allow you to hear chord progressions, programs like *Band in a Box*.

The point is that simply reading about these concepts isn't enough; you've got to *hear* them, and *use* them. You've got to swim around in the music yourself so you can *feel* the difference between Gypsy Jazz and Hard Bop, and *feel* what it's like to mess around with these progressions, these notes, these styles. That's the only way all this theory will make sense. You've got to *own* these concepts, and the only way to do that is to get them in your ears and under your fingers. Actually *in* your body. To do that you need some way to play *and* hear the harmonies, melodies, and concepts we'll be covering in the book.

You've got to have a basic ability on your instrument, too. You should have tone production and fingering and range and dynamic control down to at least an advanced beginner's level. If you're struggling with the instrument, it'll make getting these concepts under your fingers more difficult. But you've got to practice something, right? And the stuff you'll learn in this book is a rich source of practice material, for sure. A lifetime's worth, really.

It almost goes without saying that the computer is one of the most useful tools for the modern musician. Programs like *Band in a Box* and *Audacity* will take your playing, listening and your understanding to higher levels. An Internet connection is the other major tool. In a few clicks you can have access to lessons and information and video and audio that were simply unavailable even ten years ago. In fact, the computer is such an important tool, a couple chapters of *Basic Jazz Theory, volume 3* are devoted to it exclusively.

Other helpful things are curiosity, perseverance, and a willingness to experiment with your horn. Another vastly important trait is a willingness to try anything and to fail spectacularly and not let it concern you. Failing means you're pushing your limits, which means you're learning. If you're not taking lessons, I'd highly recommend it. Getting a regular source of feedback is probably *the* best way to learn quickly.

Basic Jazz Theory, volume 1: The Big Picture

Chapters in *Basic Jazz Theory, volume 1* are is short, well-paced, and as simple as possible. At the end of each chapter is a short quiz so you can test how well you've absorbed the stuff in the chapter. In addition to the review, each chapter has practical use exercises and suggestions for ear training so that you can get these concepts into your ears and heart, where they belong.

The eight chapters are ordered so that they build on each other. For example, to understand concepts in Chapter 7: *Extension Chords*, you need to know what came in chapters 5 and 6. The first and last chapters are stand-alones and can be read at any time. In fact, you might want to first read Chapter 8: *Listen and Learn*, because it's all about listening to and finding great recordings.

Icons In The Book:

Improvise Now

There's absolutely no reason to wait until you've got a bunch of theoretical knowledge in your head before actually *playing jazz*, which is to say *improvising*. That would be like owning a Ferrari, but keeping it in the garage, refusing to drive it until you learn how to take the engine apart and put it back together. That's crazytalk! This icon represents exercises to get you started and contains many useful suggestions to get you messing around with sound. Improv is where the fun is!

Brain Boosters

It can be a challenge to remember all the things in this book, but there are tricks to help with most. This icon can be found next to strategies that will help you remember important aspects of jazz theory.

Theory Geek Alert

You'll see this goofy guy when it's important to know certain facts about music theory. You'll find this icon next to information that is particularly useful and/or helpful.

Notice!

After 30 years of playing and 20 years of teaching, I've learned there are certain aspects of playing and music theory that are troublesome and tend to trip people up. This Icon is to alert you that this information should receive a little extra attention so you don't mess up.

What's Inside: The Details

Chapter 0: The Chapter Everyone Skips

You're reading it. Basic info, not entirely necessary, but it's good to have an idea what you're getting yourself into....

Chapter 1: Tune Up

A beautiful melody is a joy to play. All the theory you'll ever learn or need is embedded *right there* in those great melodies. The sooner you get them by heart, the sooner you'll have the practical aspects of all that theory for your very own. Every melody you memorize is a gem that nobody can ever take away from you. But wait, there's more! Most good players say that they have the melody in their head when they're improvising. It helps you keep your place and gives you the flavor of the tune so that whatever improvised dish you cook up yourself, it'll go with the melody.

Chapter 2: Major Scales

If melodies are the genetic material of jazz, then scales are the DNA, and the major scale in particular is an important base pair, if you'll allow me to stretch the analogy to the breaking point. The major scale is used as a reference for all kinds of things, like intervals, chords, and even other scales, all of which are covered in the coming chapters. It's crucial to know them, to know about them, and to have them under your fingers.

Chapter 3: Going Modal

Modes are a type of scale that have a close relationship with another scale. The modes this chapter covers are associated with the major scale. Modes are very important because they're associated with very common chords and chord progressions in jazz. And if you're interested in playing modal jazz, they are, as you might guess, essential.

Chapter 4: Interval Training

When you talk about written music, you need a way to explain relationships between notes, and intervals are one way to do this. If you don't know intervals, listening to someone talk about music can be like listening to a scientist talk about an experiment using degrees Kelvin. It doesn't really make sense unless you know the measurement unit. Learning about intervals is crucial to understanding chords, chord extensions, and the blues scale, covered in the following chapters. Intervals are pretty simple and this chapter will teach you what you need to know.

Chapter 5: Cutting the Chords

A chord is three or more tones sounding at the same time and it's chords that give a piece of music its feel: happy, sad, energetic, or just about any other emotion, and probably some that can't be described with words, only felt; chords provide the forward motion in a tune. In this chapter you'll learn about how to build chords, how to listen for them, and how chords in one key are related to each other. This chapter will also teach you how to read the symbols that go along with chord changes.

Chapter 6: Extension Chords

Chords in music are usually more complex and interesting than simple triads. When we stack more notes on top of the triad, these are called extensions and they obey simple rules, most of which you'll learn in this chapter. Chord extensions enhance functional harmony and increase the complex flavor of chord progressions. If you're going to play jazz, you've got to know about chord extensions and how to read them.

Chapter 7: Pentatonic and Blues Scales

There are many, many scales to learn, and the blues scale is one of the most important because jazz is suffused with the blues. The scale is very similar to a minor pentatonic scale, so this chapter will introduce pentatonic scales and then the blues scale. Blues scales are associated with particular major scales, and you'll learn about these in this chapter, too.

Chapter 8: Listen & Learn

This interlude takes listening to the next step. The listening tips you've gotten so far are like riding an exercise bicycle in the gym to get yourself in shape. Good for you, and helpful, and sort of related to real bike-riding, but not really all that fun. The kind of listening I'm talking about in this chapter is like taking a mountain bike ride on a forest trail to see the country, smell the smells and explore. Way more fun! I'm talking about listening to fantastic recordings made by world-class jazz musicians, and the importance of listening to live music. Learn about listening here and find great albums and musicians in several jazz styles.

Codicil

In the back section you'll find a book index so you can locate specific topics within the book, scales (major, natural minor, blues), and a piano keyboard and guitar fretboard that will help you understand jazz theory concepts in this book. Also included are some practice aids, all of which can also be found for free at the *Basic Jazz Theory* web site.

Get Bonus Material for the Book

Go to www.sol-ut.com to get more material that goes with this book. You can find more scales, printable practice aids, as well as printable material from this book, too, like the keyboard and guitar fingerboard in the back of the book. Click on the *Basic Jazz Theory* book, then click on the "Free Stuff" button. Enjoy!

CHAPTER 1

TUNE UP

Heard melodies are sweet, but those unheard are sweeter.

~ John Keats

In This Chapter

- Why Learn Melodies?
- By Rote or by Note?
- Memorization Strategies
- Les Yeux Noirs (Dark Eyes)

Terms to Know

- **standard:** a tune most jazz musicians know and play with some regularity.
- **super-standard:** a tune *all* jazz players know or should know.
- **fake book:** a songbook containing standards: their melodies and chord progressions.
- **tag:** used to end a tune. The last phrase is repeated 3 times.

WHY SHOULD YOU LEARN TUNES FIRST?

All aspects of music theory and jazz theory can be traced back to melody. It's what we really want to hear, and it's because of melodies that important harmonic concepts work the way they do. In some cases, melodies—and especially the chord progressions related to those melodies—are absolutely essential to building your jazz skills. More on this later.

A better reason to learn tunes first is that they can be simple, easy to memorize and fun to play. The added bonus is that you'll be able to perform right away. Think about it. If you memorize scales first, who's going to want to listen to that? I can tell you that your only listeners will be parents, spouses, or someone who wants to sell you something, and even *they* won't be interested long. Melodies are *much* more interesting, both for you and the listener.

There are even better reasons to learn tunes first, especially if you want to learn jazz theory and improvising. Most musicians (most of the good ones, anyway) often say that they keep the melody in their heads as they improvise. This not only allows you to keep track of where you are in the chord progression, it allows you to craft improvisations that are relevant to the original melody. It can take pretty sophisticated listening skills to perceive this, and most of us are probably aware of it only on a subconscious level, but the first step toward doing it yourself is memorizing melodies. Altering a melody you know by heart is another great way to start improvising with baby steps (as opposed to *Giant Steps*, a Coltrane standard).

The melodies that many jazz musicians know and love to play are called *standards*, and there are thousands of them. Among those standards are tunes I call *super-standards*, because literally everyone knows them either because they're incredible melodies or the chord progression is used in dozens of other tunes; *I Got Rhythm* is probably the best example of a super-standard.

Learning standards is one of the things any halfway decent jazz musician must do. The first step is learning the tune in its standard key signature. That's all we'll deal with for now. In later volumes of *Basic Jazz Theory* we'll take learning tunes to the next step, which is learning chord progressions and then learning melodies and chord progressions all other key signatures.

HOW TO LEARN TUNES: BY ROTE OR BY NOTE?

There are as many ways to go about learning tunes as there are people doing it. There is no one foolproof way. What's best is to incorporate all of the stuff below in whatever way makes sense to you. Whatever keeps you playing, and interested in playing, is what you want to do. Basically, you've got two options: learning tunes by ear or using the sheet music. Both are important and you should be able to do both, though in my opinion it's more valuable to learn tunes by ear. Focus on whichever skill needs attention the most. For a long time now I've focused on learning only by ear because for decades (yes, decades) I learned only from the written page. I can safely say that this is not a good balance. Do both. Practice to your weakness.

LEARN TUNES BY EAR

Music is about thinking in sound, and it can be more difficult to do this if you're struggling with written music. The strange thing is that if you're a fluent reader, the page can actually get in the way, between you and the Music. Much better for you and your music is to learn how to play songs by ear. This is the jazz tradition anyway, and it's what all the greats say you should do. They call it *learning on the bandstand*. Of course, most of those cats could read their keisters off, so don't neglect the reading skills. Just make sure you practice playing along with only your ears. A live setting is best, but tunes you like are even better, because you really *know* them; they're in your ear and you have them by heart. This is important because as you're trying to figure out how to play a melody, you'll have to compare it to your memory of the tune. And if you're playing along with that well-known melody, you have to use your ears, too.

It doesn't matter if it's a *Beatles* tune, the latest *Black Eyed Peas* single, a classic from U2, or one of Merle Haggard's hits. Learning tunes by ear will help build the skills you'll need for all kinds of listening, including the kind of listening you do when you improvise. I recommend learning all these tunes by ear if you can. If you're not used to this it can be *very* difficult, time-consuming, and without patience, a little frustrating. That's how it feels when you're getting better at things. Keep at it. Pick simple songs to start out with like the ones in this chapter.

LEARN TUNES WITH WRITTEN MUSIC

If you know how to read music, this is can be a great option. In fact, you should be able to do both. If you're weak in one area, focus on that. Because I learned by reading only for a long time, I now try to learn *everything* by ear in order to make up for my lack in that area. If I'm pressed for time, or performing a song that isn't quite in the little gray cells yet, I'll use the written music. The danger with written music is that you can be seduced into always using it and never memorize the music. This is a handicap because without the written music in front of you, you've got nothing. If you choose to use written music, get rid of the page as soon as you can. This means memorizing.

There is another reason to get rid of the written music as quickly as you can. Your brain has a limited amount of processing power and if you're spending that power on reading from the page, you have less resources for listening and responding, which is what jazz is all about. If you can read music, by all means, use that valuable skill to your advantage, but don't rely on the page. Get rid of it as soon as possible. Reduce your cognitive load. I'm repeating myself because this is important. Relying on the written music would be like keeping the training wheels on your bike as you compete in the Tour de France. People will snicker and believe you're not to be taken seriously because you still don't get it. Nobody wants that.

MEMORIZING

A jazz musician who hasn't memorized tunes is like a chef without ingredients. Memorizing melodies is important if you want to play jazz at any level. Think about it. How many musicians (besides classical) have you seen with music on the stage? Not many. Memorized tunes are essential for jam sessions, for improvising, and for *owning* a piece of music. In fact, memorizing is so important, it gets its own section just after this list of tunes to memorize.

TUNE LIST

This is a topic of endless discussion among jazz musicians, and musicians of any genre. What are the essential tunes? If you were stranded on a desert island, what jazz tunes would you want in your memory? Or more realistically, if you went to a jam session with musicians you admired, what tunes would you want under your belt? Clearly, this list is different for everyone, but there *are* tunes that just about everyone knows (I call 'em *superstandards*). The list I've compiled below is many hundred tunes short of comprehensive and represents tunes I like. They have simple, "sticky," melodies, are relatively easy, and are fun to play. It's a great place to start but you should keep an ear out for tunes that speak to you or that musicians in your area call out in jam sessions.

Learning tunes is one of the more fun and rewarding parts of playing jazz. Learning these tunes will get you working on all sorts of more advanced concepts in the most practical way. You may not know what standard American song form, 32 bar song form, or AABA song form are (they're all usually the same thing), but by learning the tunes below, you'll be learning it by *doing* it, much better than a theoretical understanding. Applying the theory of song form will come later. You don't need to know anything about song form to play a beautiful melody. So, here are my selections for you. I've chosen only fifteen easy tunes because it's best to start slowly. In following volumes I'll add more and more suggestions of tunes to learn including some very difficult ones. For now, go with the easy stuff.

As you listen to more and more jazz, you'll begin to run across tunes that make you say, "I *have* to learn that tune!" Those are the tunes you want to focus on. Because I'm a trumpet player, there are a lot of trumpet players on the list. There are *many* other recordings of all of these tunes. Talk to your teacher or other players for more examples. If you follow along with written music, you'll notice that musicians rarely (I'm tempted to say *never*) play the melody as it's written. They make the melody their own by changing rhythms, inflections, and often even the notes themselves.

Fake books with the written music for these tunes and the recordings I've mentioned as well as others can be found at www.BasicJazzTheory.com

15 Easy Jazz Melodies to Learn Now

Title	Composer	Artist (Album)
All Blues	Miles Davis	Miles Davis (*Kind of Blue*)
All the Things You Are	Jerome Kern	Ella Fitzgerald (*Love Songs-Best Verve Songbook*)
Autumn Leaves	Kosma/Mercer	Miles Davis/Cannonball Adderley (*Somethin' Else*) Eva Cassidy's beautiful version w/ lyrics: http://tiny.cc/ikzvz
Blue Monk	Thelonius Monk	John Coltrane/Monk (*Live @ Carnegie Hall*)
Caravan	Juan Tizol	Cootie Williams (*Cootie Williams in HiFi*)
Dark Eyes (Les Yeux Noirs)	traditional	Lagrene/Rosenberg/Shmitt (http://tiny.cc/fbvpn) Getz/Gillespie (*Artistry of Stan Getz: Verve, disc 2*)
Work Song	Nat Adderley	Nat Adderley (*Work Song*)
It Don't Mean a Thing (If it Ain't Got That Swing)	Duke Ellington	Dizzy Gillespie & Stan Getz (*Diz & Getz*)
Mack the Knife	Weill/Brecht	Louis Armstrong (*Definitive Louis Armstrong*)
My Funny Valentine	Rogers/Hart	Chet Baker (*Deep in a Dream: The Ultimate Chet Baker Collection*, trk 1=instrumental, trk 2=vocal)
Rhythm-ning	Thelonius Monk	Gerry Mulligan/Monk (*Mulligan Meets Monk*)
Softly as In a Morning Sunrise	Romberg/ Hammerstein II	Sonny Rollins (*Live at the Village Vanguard*)
The Blues Walk	Clifford Brown	Clifford Brown (*Clifford Brown & Max Roach*)
The Girl from Ipanema	Antonio C. Jobim	Getz/Gilberto(s) (*Getz & Gilberto*)
What is This Thing Called Love	Cole Porter	Clifford Brown (*Clifford Brown & Max Roach at Basin Street*)

Memorizing Tunes

On Dizzy Gillespie's album *Rhythmstick*, they left the tape rolling as the musicians warmed up. Phil Woods, the alto player, noodles around, then stops and says "Remember this one?" and he launches into a Charlie Parker tune called *Barbados*. Before he finishes two phrases, the bass player, Charlie Haden, jumps in; Marvin "Smitty" Smith on drums jumps in before the first section is over; then all the rest come in at the bridge and off they go.

Barbados is an example of a standard that many jazz musicians know. Most professional jazz musicians can play many hundreds if not thousands of tunes at a moment's notice, in any key. Though the melodies are always different, the chord progressions and form of the song are often very similar or identical, but this won't be clear to you until you *own* a tune. To do that, learn a bunch of melodies and discover (meaning *hear*) the similarities for yourself. The only way is to memorize.

Memorizing is a skill just like any other, and there are strategies to make it easier. These are based on real-world reports of musicians memorizing music, and they work. We'll touch on more advanced techniques for memorizing as you get more savvy about your jazz theory, but for now, here are some basic pointers to help improve your memorization skills. If you're interested, check out a cool book by Gary Sudnow, *Ways of the Hand*, a book about learning to play jazz piano. Also helpful might be a book called *Practicing Perfection: Memory and Piano Performance*, by Chaffin, Imreh, and Crawford. It's research on how a pianist memorizes music. Though it deals with classical music, there are many helpful tips in the book.

Here are some suggestions for memorizing the tunes on the above list and *Dark Eyes*, a tune I've included in this chapter for you to learn.

THE BIG PICTURE

Don't just bang away on a song over and over until you hammer it into your memory. That's a long process and is only used by beginners who don't know any better. The first thing to do to memorize quickly is to get the big picture of the tune in mind. It's like the difference between looking at a map before you go out into the woods and just wandering off into the forest. One way is smarter. Getting an idea of the big picture will help give the tune a structure in your head which you can then use to support the melody. Here are some tips:

1. Listen to a good version of the tune many times. If it has lyrics, learn them and sing, hum, and/or whistle along (extra credit: find 2+ different versions and compare). When musicians take solos, sing/hum/whistle the melody during the improvisation. Can you follow?

2. Notice how the melody rises and falls, where it repeats, where it changes, its speed, its meter, its feel, especially where and when the original melody returns and anything else you perceive with your ears.

3. Find the sheet music for the song (for best learning, transcribe the melody by ear w/ your axe). Notice in the music notation the same things as you heard above: repetitions, key signatures, melody contour, meter, speed, and anything else you perceive with your eyes.

4. As you listen, draw a sound map of the tune. This doesn't require music notation, but if you're familiar with it, go for it (often helpful with repeats). Show melodic contour, repeated sections, or any other aspect of the music that speaks to you. Translating the music you hear into a form you can see is tricky, but a good way to help burn the tune into your memory. As you get better at memorizing, you can do all this mentally. Learning more about jazz theory will help.

THE NITTY GRITTY

You can take the following steps at the same time you work through the above, but ideally, you should have the melody of the tune in your head already. This is essential if you're trying to figure it out by ear!

1. Play the song on your axe at a tempo that is slow enough to make it easy. Write in fingerings if you need it. If you're playing along and the tune is fast, use a program like Audacity to slow down the original (find out how to do this in *BJT vol. 3*).

2. Choose one section of the song and learn only that section, phrase-by-phrase. Try to choose the section that repeats (most songs have a lot of repetition). For a song that has AABA form (as *most* are--more on this in *BJT vol. 2*), start with the A section and memorize that first. That way you've already got 3/4 of the tune down. Make it beautiful (especially important if you're doing this from the written page). Listen to many versions.

3. Repeat this for each new/different section until you've got all the sections memorized, then combine them to put the whole tune together. As it's memorized, have the music handy for

nudging your memory, but don't rely on it. Play along with a recording at this stage if you can. Play along while the soloists take their solos, too (this can be challenging).

4 While you're away from the instrument, do the fingering of the tune while you sing/hum/whistle it. Visualize the music or the sound map you created above while you go through the tune in your mind.

5 Perform the melody for someone. This added pressure can reveal flaws in your memory because it can be more difficult to remember things when you're under pressure. Choose a setting that won't stress you out too much (like for a loved one), and work your way up to performances with more pressure (an open mic at a local cafe, or Carnegie Hall).

A Tune to memorize: *Les Yeux Noirs (Dark Eyes)*

Up next is one of my favorite tunes, *Les Yeux Noirs (Dark Eyes)*. It's a Gypsy Jazz standard and you can hear burning examples by Django Reinhardt, Stochello Rosenberg, Birelli Lagrene, and a whole host of others. It's from an old Russian lullaby, sped up to breakneck tempo.

A bass clef version can be found on the next page, as well as the D harmonic minor scale to be used for improvising over the chords. We won't cover this scale until *BJT vol. 2*, but there's no reason not to start now. There's a fantastic version of this tune with Dizzy Gillespie on trumpet and Stan Getz playing tenor sax on *The Artistry of Stan Getz: The Verve Years, volume 2*. I just discovered it and am excited. It's 12 minutes long!

This music is in concert pitch. Free, printable versions for trumpet, clarinet, saxes, and other non-C instruments can be found at www.BasicJazzTheory.com

Les Yeux Noirs (Dark Eyes)

FAST

Scale to use for improvising on Dark Eyes: D harmonic minor

Ear Training

1. Listening to masters will help you more than *anything* else! Go to accujazz.com and start exploring. Make a note of recordings, artists, and styles that you really like. Order the album. You can find all the albums in this book and many, many more at www.BasicJazzTheroy.com.

2. Go to Pandora.com and create radio stations based on the following artists: Louis Armstrong, Duke Ellington, Count Basie, Ella Fitzgerald, Billie Holliday, Dexter Gordon, Lester Young, Sonny Rollins, Roy Eldridge, Clifford Brown, Lee Morgan, Miles Davis, Freddie Hubbard, Dizzy Gillespie, Charlie Parker, J.J. Johnson, Django Reinhardt, Wes Montgomery, Joe Pass, Kenny Burrell, Bobby Broom, Oscar Peterson, Art Tatum, Thelonius Monk, Ray Brown, Christian McBride, Tito Puente, Ray Barretto, Ed Thigpen and any others you like or have heard of. These are just the ones at the tip of my brain. There are many others who are also fantastic. Start listening now.

3. Go to over to http://shuffler.fm/ and scroll right to find the jazz "channel." This will take you to blogs from which you can listen and learn about jazz and jazz-inflected music. A fun site and as you can see, it can be a source for exploring *many* styles of music. Props to the Intertubes!

CHAPTER REVIEW

1. What is a jazz standard?

2. Name three Internet sites where you can listen to jazz music for free.

3. What is a sound map?

4. Why should you consider the "big picture" of a tune when memorizing it?

5. Why sing the melody during a recorded solo, or have it in your head while improvising?

1. A jazz tune that all/most musicians know and can play.

2. accujazz.com, pandora.com, shufflr.fm, musicovery.com, others...

3. Graphic representation of music; shows shape, contour, color, texture, etc. Music notation not required.

4. Makes memorizing easier. You can spot where the melody repeats, changes. Gives structure to the melody.

5. Keeps your place in the chord progression. Allows your solo to take on the "flavor" of the tune itself.

PRACTICAL USE

1. Take one of the standards from the list above and sit down with both the recording and the sheet music. Memorize the tune. Compare the melodies as they're written with the melodies as they're played. If you have trouble hearing the music when you're reading it, be sure to choose a tune you've learned so you can hear how the artist makes the melody unique. Miles Davis was a master of this, so he'd be a good choice, but everyone does it.

2. Choose another tune from the list and as you memorize it, alter it in ways that are pleasing to you. Toy with it. Experiment. Listen to the masters. Don't take the written page as some literal, sacred document. Try changing single notes, alter rhythms, chop up long notes with tonguing, extend notes beyond their notated marking (you'll have to shorten others to make up for this lengthening). Record yourself so you can evaluate your results later. When you're not focused on playing, you can focus more intently (and critically) on listening.

CHAPTER 2

MAJOR SCALES

Success on any major scale requires you to accept responsibility.... In the final analysis, the one quality that all successful people have...is the ability to take on responsibility.

~ Michael Korda

In This Chapter

- Major Scale Anatomy
- Whole/Half Step Patterns
- C Major
- Maj Scales with Sharps
- Maj Scales with Flats

Terms to Know

- Half step: the shortest distance between notes in Western music. Two adjacent keys on a piano.
- Whole step: the second-shortest distance between 2 notes in Western music. Two half steps
- Flat: lowers a pitch by a half step.
- Sharp: raises a pitch by a half step.
- Natural: cancels the effect of a sharp/flat

THE MAJOR SCALE

The major scale is the basis for nearly all music you're familiar with, from country to hip-hop, classical to jazz, grunge to punk and beyond. Other scales are often described based on their relationships to the major scale. Intervals—the measurement of distance between two notes—are based on the major scale. Chord symbols are derived from the major scale. It's a useful scale to know. Our somewhat musty definition of a scale is: *a graduated series of musical tones ascending or descending in order of pitch according to a specific scheme of their intervals.*

With the chromatic scale—you know, every consecutive note on piano—the scheme of intervals is half steps. With the major scale, the scheme of intervals is a series of whole and half steps. Remember that a whole step consists of two half steps.

Just like chords, every scale has a letter name and a descriptive name. The letter name is the bottom note of the scale (also root or fundamental). The descriptive name tells you what kind of scale it is, like major, minor, blues, pentatonic, etc. For example, the D Major scale would start on D and end on D and have the necessary whole and half steps that make up a major scale.

The example scale we'll use will be the C Major scale, because it has no sharps or flats in it. Use the keyboard in the back of the book (or better yet, a real one) to follow along and you'll understand these concepts more quickly and more thoroughly. Remember, though, understanding is next-to-nothing! You must *hear* these things. Play them on your instrument or a piano. Get the sound in your ears.

The C Major Scale

Before I show you the scale, I've got to define a couple images which are used to show half and whole steps. They're simple, and a good visual reference.

half step: /\   whole step: ☐

If you have access to an actual keyboard, play the scale below. It will be all white notes from C to C. If you don't know the note names on the piano, check the codicil in the back of this book for the piano keyboard template and make some stickers for your piano 'til you've got 'em down. Do you recognize the sound of this scale?

Staff 2.1   The C Major Scale. Ascending whole and half steps shown.

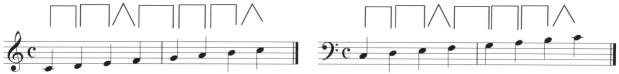

Whole and Half Steps for the Major Scale

There is a naturally occurring half step between E-F and B-C (no sharp or flat sign is needed for natural half-steps). In the C Major scale, these natural half steps give us the pattern of whole and half steps without the bother of accidentals.

As you can see above, the pattern for the C major scale: *whole, whole, half, whole, whole, whole, half (wwhwwwh)*. You'll need to memorize this, because this pattern of whole and half steps is the same for *every* major scale.

Octave

This is as good a place as any to introduce you to the *octave*, a type of interval which contains a certain amount of notes. Like octopus and octagon, the octave also has an 8 in it.

Look at the scale above, and count the notes from C to C. There are 8 of them. That's an octave: 8 diatonic notes. From one letter name to the next, either up or down, is an octave. If you measure with half steps, an octave is 12 half steps.

Scales with Accidentals

Now we can take that pattern of whole and half steps and apply it to another scale. Let's start on F this time.

F Major Scale

Staff 2.2   The F major scale, ascending, with whole and half steps shown.

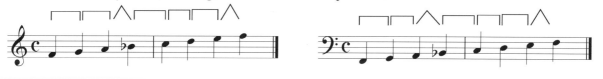

In order for our series of whole and half steps to be correct (wwhwwwh), we have to alter a note. Look at your keyboard while you examine the whole and half steps in the F major scale to see where those half and whole steps fall. That Bb is necessary to get the half step between the third and fourth *degrees* of the scale. The Bb also gives us the whole step between the fourth and fifth degrees of the scale.

A degree is a name for a scale tone, and is usually associated with a number. For example the 4th degree of a scale is the fourth note from the bottom. The bottom note is always "1," also known as the *tonic*. In the F major scale above scale, because E to F is a natural half step, we don't need to alter either of those degrees of the scale to have the half step between the seventh and eighth degrees of the scale.

G Major Scale

Staff 2.3   The G major scale, ascending, with whole and half steps shown.

Follow along with your keyboard and you can see where the whole and half steps should be for the Major scale starting on G.

Between the third and fourth degree of the scale we have the natural half step from B-C, and between the seventh and eighth degree of the scale, in order to have a half step, we need an F#. And it just so happens that between the sixth and seventh degree of this scale we need a whole step; E to F# is a whole step.

Major Scales with Many Accidentals

This same technique can be applied to a scale with any starting note. Just for kicks, we'll do one with lots of flats and one with lots of sharps. You'll need to follow along with your keyboard for this one, so have it ready.

A Major Scale with Lots of Flats

Staff 2.4   The Db major scale, ascending, whole and half steps shown.

A Major Scale with Lots of Sharps

Staff 2.5   The F# major scale, ascending, whole and half steps shown.

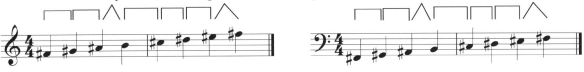

More Enharmonics

Take a look at the seventh degree of the F# major scale above. An E#, right? The enharmonic note that is the same pitch as E# is F. It's that natural half step between E and F that causes this. Similarly, B# is the same pitch as C. Use your keyboard to help with your understanding of this concept.

Going the other way, Fb is the same pitch as E, and Cb is the same pitch as B. These facts will be handy later when you start spelling out chords in keys w/ many flats or sharps.

EAR TRAINING

1. Sing a major scale. If you have trouble, play along with piano or a partner while you match the pitches with your voice. Do this 'til you can sing it without help.

2. Use the scale patterns in the Codicil of this book (page 66). Play and sing them.

3. Listen carefully for the difference between the whole and the half step. Sing a whole step. Sing a half step. Sing along with a piano or a partner if this is difficult. The half step in the major scale comes between the 3rd and 4th degrees and the 7th and 8th degrees. Can you hear the difference?

4. This one requires two players: one to play and another to listen. One person plays two notes either a whole step or a half step apart. The second person identifies which it is. If you don't have a partner but do have an internet connection, go to: www.musictheory.net/exercises. You can customize the listening test to include only whole and half steps.

IMPROVISE NOW

1. Play around with the major scale that is easiest for you. There is no such thing as a mistake (you were only trying something). Choose a note to repeat frequently and come back to it often. Repeat short ideas. Repeat longer ideas. Vary articulations.

2. With a partner, choose a scale to play and improvise together. Don't just randomly play the notes, though; listen to each other and try to respond musically so you have a musical conversation. Try sustaining notes together and move to different notes together. Have one person sustain while the other moves, then switch. Use your imagination to change it up.

SOMETHIN' ELSE

If you understand the major scale, you've got a powerful tool to unlock the intricacies of much of music theory, and this goes double for jazz theory. If you haven't already, memorize all 12 major scales on your instrument. All major scales are in the back of this book and printable at BasicJazzTheory.com. Better yet, figure them out by ear and memorize them that way. Major scales are essential for understanding the information in the next chapter which covers modes. The modes we'll cover are based on the major scale. Important and useful for improvising.

For an added challenge, play your major scales around the circle of fourths (in the Codicil).

CHAPTER REVIEW

1. What is an octave?

2. What is the series of whole and half steps for the major scale?

3. What is the symbol for a half step?

4. What is the symbol for a whole step?

5. Between which degrees of the major scale do the half steps occur?

6. Can you sing, hum, and/or whistle a major scale?

1. The distance from one note to the next note with the same letter name. Twelve half steps or 6 whole steps.

2. wwhwwwh

3. ∧

4. ⊓

5. 3-4, 7-8

6. Keep at it until you can answer, "Yes!"

PRACTICAL USE

1. On a blank staff using the clef of your instrument, write in an E-flat low on the staff. Use your keyboard to figure out the E-flat major scale. Write it down, then play it on your instrument. Does is sound right? Sing it.

2. Do the same thing, starting on A. Play and sing the scale until it's memorized. Make it musical!

3. Write out all 12 Major scales below. If you don't know them figure them out based on the information in this chapter. Use your keyboard (a real one if you have it...).

CHAPTER 3

GOING MODAL

Just because you know umpteen billion scales, it doesn't mean you have to use them all in a solo.

~ Kirk Hammett

In This Chapter

- Basic Mode Info
- Mode Relation to Major Scale
- How to Find a Mode in Keys Other than C
- Modes From Other Scales
- Ear Training
- Chapter Review

Terms to Know

- Mode: A type of scale.
- Modal Jazz: A jazz style, begun in the late 1950's and early 1960's. Focused on improvisation. Led by Miles Davis.
- lid: hat. "That dude Pres is sportin' a nice lid."
- popsicle stick: a sax or clarinet player's reed.
- smokin': playing your butt off. "Wes Montgomery was smokin' at the Half Note."

WHAT IS A MODE?

A mode is a type of scale. Modes are used in most types of music, like salsa, jazz, country, rock, fusion, speed metal, Indian ragas (though it's used in a different way) and more. To find out the details, read on.

The two modes which have been used the most, and the only two most people know, are now called the Major and natural minor scales. Their original names were the *Ionian mode* (Major), and the *Aeolian mode* (natural minor). The other modes are: *Dorian, Phrygian, Lydian, Mixolydian,* and *Locrian*. Don't ask me why they're capitalized.

Modes are easy to understand. We'll map out each mode's series of whole and half steps and use the key of C so there aren't any sharps or flats to bother with. Remember about the natural half steps between E and F, and B and C.

THE MODES

These modes are based on the major scale. Later we'll talk about modes based on other scales. Basically, there are 7 modes in every key signature, major or minor. The major and minor scales are just another type of mode (called Ionian and Aeolian). We'll use the major scale to talk about all the other modes in this chapter. For example, if you play an octave scale starting from the 2nd note of a major scale, you've played the Dorian mode. Confused? Read on.

IONIAN

As you already know, the Ionian mode is the same as the C Major scale. All the white keys on the piano from C to C. The whole-half step pattern is WWHWWWH.

Ionian is used in nearly all Western music, from Acid Jazz to Zydeco.

DORIAN

The Dorian mode begins on the second degree of the Major scale and in the key of C goes from D to D on the white keys of the piano. The pattern of whole and half steps is WHWWWHW. This scale goes with ii chords, minor chords and minor 7th chords (you'll learn all these details about chords soon!). Why is this scale is associated with the ii chord? If you start on the 2nd degree (there's the ii) of the major scale and play an octave, you'll have this scale. The chord built from this scale is the ii chord. We'll get to chords later in this book.

Just like any scale or more, there are 12 Dorians, corresponding to the 12 key signatures. The Dorian mode is a minor-sounding scale used in rock, jazz, blues, fusion and many other genres.

PHRYGIAN

You've probably caught on to the pattern by now. Phrygian begins on the third degree of the Major scale and in the key of C is E to E on the white keys of the piano. The whole-half step pattern is HWWWHWW.

This mode has a Spanish flavor and is used in jazz, flamenco music, fusion, and speed metal. Twelve of these, too. In fact, there are 12 of each type of mode because there are 12 different key signatures.

LYDIAN

Lydian begins on the 4th degree of the Major scale and in the key of C is from F to F on the white keys of the piano. Whole-half step pattern is WWWHWWH.

You might see this mode in jazz, fusion, rock, or country music. It's like a major scale with a raised 4th which gives this scale an odd sound. Lydian mode ascending.

MIXOLYDIAN

Mixolydian begins on the fifth degree of the Major scale, and in the key of C is G to G on the white keys. Whole-half step pattern is WWHWWHW.

This mode shows up in jazz, rockabilly, country, blues, and rock.

 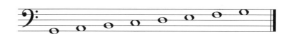

AEOLIAN

Also known as the natural minor scale, the Aeolian mode begins on the sixth degree of the Major scale. In the key of C it's from A to A on the white keys. WHWWHWW.

This mode appears in all kinds of music: jazz, pop, country, Rock, blues, heavy metal, classical, and on and on.

LOCRIAN

The Locrian mode has a very exotic and other-worldly sound. All because of the placement of those half steps. You'll find Locrian in fusion and in jazz.

The Locrian mode begins on the seventh degree of the Major scale, and is B to B in the key of C.

 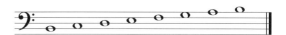

Finding Modes in Other Keys

There are two ways to find a mode in another key. You can find a mode within a certain key signature, or find a mode starting on a specific note. To find a mode in a certain key is easiest. Just a couple steps.

1. Play the Major scale in the key you'll be using. For an example, let's say you wanted to find the Dorian mode which uses the key of Ab. First step is to play the Ab Major scale.

2. Depending on the mode you want, start on the appropriate note in the Major scale and play an octave in the key of the Major scale. In our example, the Dorian mode begins on the second degree of the Major scale, a Bb. Bb Dorian is Bb to Bb in the key of Ab.

To find a mode beginning on a specific note, the process is a little different but still pretty simple.

1. Depending on the mode you want, find out which major scale has that note in the appropriate place. Let's stick with Dorian for an example. You want to find the Dorian mode which begins on F. So you'd find out which Major scale has F as its second note. The answer is Eb.

2. Then use the key signature you found in step 1 for the Dorian mode. In our example, you'd play F to F using the key of Eb.

3. Another option is to use the pattern of whole and half steps associated with the mode you want.

Modes Using Other Scales

Modes are also built from other scales, like the ascending melodic minor scale. This produces some interesting and exotic sounding scales. And the names are pretty wild, too. Like the Lydian augmented mode, the Lydian dominant mode, the half-diminished (also called Locrian #2), and the diminished whole tone mode.

These modes deal with more advanced harmonic practices, and I've included them to show you that there is more to learn once you've mastered the modes of the major scale. There is always something more to practice, something more to learn! These will be covered in BJT volume

| melodic minor (ascending) | Lydian augmented | half-diminished or Locrian #2 |

Ear Training

1. Take one major scale that you're learning, and play all the modes associated with it. While you're learning, *really listen* to hear how the mode sounds. Learn to sing and recognize the Dorian and Mixolydian modes. In addition to the Ionian (major scale), these are the most-used modes in jazz.

2. With partners: Use the Dorian, Mixolydian, and Ionian (major) modes. Appoint one person as leader. The leader switches between these three modes and the others have to listen to hear when the leader switches. It's okay (in fact it's great!) if you use eye contact and/or head nods to indicate when you change. Jazz musicians often communicate this way, so get used to it now.

IMPROVISE NOW

1. Play the 1st, 3rd, and 5th degrees of the scale/mode, then improvise using all the notes. Come back often to the 1st, 3rd, 5th scale degrees. Emphasize the root note (1st note) when improvising. *Really listen* to the quality of the sound.

2. Partners: One play plays the 1st, 3rd, and 5th degrees of the mode you're working on over and over in any rhythm. Vary from free and open rhythms to a groove. The other player improvises using the mode you're working through. Trade off. For added challenge, trade off without stopping.

SOMETHIN' ELSE

Again, modes aren't particularly necessary to understand music theory in general, but they're crucial to gain a deeper understanding of jazz theory and especially improvisation.

After the chapter review, we'll move on to intervals, which will be useful for building chords and understanding most other concepts in music theory.

CHAPTER REVIEW

1. What are the names of the modes?

2. Which mode is the same as the major scale?

3. Which mode is the same as the natural minor scale?

4. What is the starting note for the Dorian mode which uses the key of D Major?

5. What key signature would be used for the Dorian mode beginning on an A?

6. What key signature would be used for the Mixolydian mode beginning on F?

1. Ionian, Dorian, Phrygian, Lydian, Mixolydian, Aeolian, Locrian

2. Ionian

3. Aeolian

4. E

5. Key of G. One sharp

6. Key of Bb, two flats

PRACTICAL USE

1. Write out all of the modes in the key of F. Learn them on your instrument/voice. Know where the half steps are in each. Then learn all of the modes in the key of G, then B♭, then D, etc.

2. Another option is to learn only one mode at a time in every key, for example, the D Ionian, D Dorian, D Phrygian, etc.

3. What is the benefit of doing it one way over the other?

CHAPTER 4

INTERVAL TRAINING

There is no cure for birth and death save to enjoy the interval.

~ George Santayana

In This Chapter

- Intervals Defined
- Perfect Intervals
- Major Intervals
- Altering Intervals
- Minor Intervals
- Diminished Intervals
- Augmented Intervals

Terms to Know

- harmonic interval: distance between two notes sounding simultaneously.
- melodic interval: distance between notes sounding sequentially.
- compound interval: an interval greater than an octave.
- horn: any instrument, including piano or guitar (see also: axe).

INTERVALS BY THE NUMBER

An *interval* is the distance between two pitches. An interval is expressed as a number from 1 to 13. It *is* possible to use a number greater than 13, but for now we'll forget about it. In jazz you tend to see these larger numbers more often, usually 9s, 11s, and 13s. More on this during the chapter coming up on chord extensions. Intervals are essential to understanding many of the concepts in this book, and are handy when you're talking to other musicians. You might tell someone, "Yeah, the melody goes up a 7th after the G," or, "Let's add the 9th to that chord." If you don't know your intervals, you'll have no idea what your fellow musicians are talking about. As with all other concepts in this book, it's crucial for you to be able to *hear* these intervals, too.

There are two types of basic intervals, harmonic and melodic. A *harmonic interval* is when two notes are sounded simultaneously. A *melodic interval* is when two notes are sounded one after the other.

Harmonic Interval

Melodic Interval

When measuring the interval between two notes (both harmonic and melodic), the interval is always measured from the lower note to the higher.

A Simple Way to Find an Interval

To find the number of an interval, simply count every line and space from the bottom note to the top note. *Be sure to count the line/space of the bottom note as 1.* This is the most common mistake when figuring out an interval. If you don't count the bottom note as 1, you'll end up with the wrong interval.

Staff 4.6   The melodic interval of a fifth and a sixth. Notice in the second example that the count starts with the *lower note* even though it comes after the higher one. Intervals are always measured from the lower note.

Staff 4.7   The harmonic intervals of a third and a seventh. Play it. Sing it. Play/sing w/ a partner. Own it.

Interval Quality

In addition to having a number, each interval will also have a quality of *perfect, major, minor, diminished,* or *augmented.*

In order to understand these qualities, we've got to take a look at the major scale again. We'll use the key of C Major because it's the least complicated, but these principles can be applied to any key signature.

Perfect Intervals

The *Perfect* intervals are: *Unison* (the same note, also called *prime*), *4ths, 5ths,* and *octaves* (8ths). They're called perfect because the ratios of their frequencies are simple whole numbers. These sound qualities were first observed and praised in China and were first explored in the West by Pythagoras. For more information on this subject, get *Hearing and Written Music* by Ron Gorow. The symbol for a perfect interval is "P". When written, the intervals look like so:

PU/PP	perfect unison/perfect prime
P4	perfect fourth
P5	perfect fifth
P8	perfect octave

Major Intervals

All other intervals in a major scale are called major intervals. That leaves us with seconds, thirds, sixths, and sevenths. The letter used for a major interval is a *capital "M"*. These intervals would be written like so:

M2   major second

M3   major third

M6   major sixth

M7   major seventh

It takes two notes to have an interval, so in the example that follows I've put a *C* below each note, which gives us harmonic intervals up the major scale. Any of these intervals spread out one after the other would be a melodic interval.

Staff 4.8   Intervals in the key of C Major, from the root note, C.

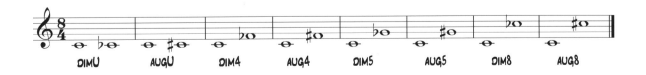

Altering Perfect Intervals

A perfect interval can be raised or lowered, and this changes the quality of the interval.
A perfect interval lowered a half step becomes a diminished interval.
A perfect interval raised a half step becomes an augmented interval.

 Here's a little diagram to help remember this. The *aug* is above the P because an augmented interval is higher than a Perfect interval. The *dim* is below the P because a diminished interval is lower than a Perfect interval.

Staff 4.9   Altered Perfect intervals from C.

ALTERING MAJOR INTERVALS

Major intervals can also be altered by raising or lowering them.
A Major interval lowered a half step becomes a minor interval.
A Major interval raised a half step becomes an augmented interval.

AUG
MAJ
MIN

Here's another little diagram. Just like before, the *aug* is above because it's higher than the Major, and the *min* is below because it's a lower than the Major:

Staff 4.10   Altered Major intervals from C.

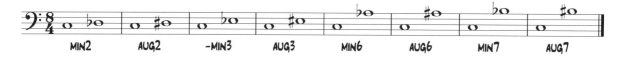

MIN2   AUG2   –MIN3   AUG3   MIN6   AUG6   MIN7   AUG7

And just to mess with your mind a little, a minor interval lowered a half step becomes a diminished interval. If you're wondering how a note which already has a flat can be lowered still further, you've forgotten about double flats. Look it up if you're curious.

FINDING AN INTERVAL

In a few easy steps you can find an interval. It's easiest with the key of C so we'll stick with that for examples, but you should be able to find an interval from any note to any other note.
Count the lines and spaces up from the lower of the two notes. Count the first as #1.

1 Determine if the number of the interval is Major or Perfect.
   (M = 2, 3, 6, 7; P = U, 4, 5, 8).

2 Determine if the interval is lowered or raised from what it would be in the Major scale.
   Use the Major scale which starts on the lower of the two notes.

For example, lets take a C and a Bb, with C being the lower of the two notes. For the first step, we count the lines and spaces to get the number of the interval.

For step 2, we need to know if a 7th is a Perfect or Major interval. It's a Major interval if unaltered. But this one is altered (lowered with a flat), so....
For step 3 we determine that the 7th has been lowered a half step, which would make it a minor 7th. If you can simply *hear* it, and play it, this is much quicker.

Intervals Greater than an Octave

So far we've only used intervals up to the number 8 (an octave). Intervals can be greater than an octave and are called compound intervals. The process of finding them is the same. Simply count up from the lower of the two notes. There will be more information and study of compound intervals in Chapter 6, Chord Extensions. Here's an example showing the interval of a ninth:

Finding Intervals in Keys Other than C

The best way to find intervals in other keys is to have all the Major scales memorized. There are only 12 of them, so it shouldn't take too long (they're in the back of this book). Because I'm originally a trumpet player, I still figure out intervals by running up the major scales with trumpet fingerings. It's sort of like counting on your fingers. Very handy (pun intended).

Another way is to memorize how many whole and half steps are in each interval. For example, there are 12 half steps in a Perfect Octave, 7 half steps in a Perfect 5th, 4 half steps in a major third, etc. Run up the chromatic scale w/ your fingers as with the major scale.

Ear Training

The trick is to sing or play each interval over and over and over until you can sing any interval from any note. There are many ways to do this.

1. Memorize tunes that have particular intervals in them. One good one that has lots of examples in it (it starts w/ an Octave), is the melody to *Over the Rainbow*, by Harold Arlen. It's got octaves, Major 6ths, minor 3rds and many more.

2. Pick an interval a week and sing/play that interval from every note you can sing/play until you've memorized the difference in pitch. Listen for it everywhere: music, speech, car horns, etc.

3. Sing intervals anywhere you can get away with it without looking weird. Of course, if you don't mind looking strange, do it everywhere): in the car, in the shower, hum them under your breath in a boring lecture or meeting, use your imagination.

4. Pick a tune from Chapter 1 and identify the intervals you hear/see in the tune. Continue with the other songs in that Chapter and any other song you know by heart.

5. With a partner, take turns playing and identifying intervals either at the piano, or on your instrument. If you're the one playing the interval, make sure you know which one you're playing so you can tell your partner if he/she got it right.

Somethin' Else

It may take some time living with these intervals before they really stick in your head. Keep at it until you've got them. Knowing your intervals will be necessary when we get to building chords, which is coming up next.

1. What is the definition of an interval?

2. What is a harmonic interval?

3. What is a melodic interval?

4. How do you find the number of an interval?

5. What will always be the number of the lower note?

6. What are the qualities of intervals?

7. What does a Perfect interval become when lowered a half step?

8. What does a Perfect interval become when raised a half step?

9. What does a Major interval become when raised a half step?

10. What does a Major interval become when lowered a half step?

11. What is this interval?

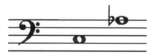

12. What is this interval?

1. The distance between two pitches

2. The distance between two pitches sounded at the same time

3. The distance between two pitches sounded one after the other

4. Count each line and space up from the lower of the two notes

5. 1

6. Perfect, Major, minor, diminished, augmented

7. diminished (dim)

8. augmented (aug or +)

9. augmented (aug or +)

10. minor

11. min 6

12. aug 4

Practical Use

1. Using a piece of music you're currently studying, identify at least four intervals. Sing and play the interval out of the context of the piece. When you play the piece from now on, be aware of the sound of the intervals you've chosen. When you can identify them by their sound and sing them (low to high; high to low; and together), pick a couple more and repeat the process.

2. Draw a whole note C on the treble or bass clef staff (any octave is fine). Draw another note a fifth above the C. What is the name of the note a fifth above C? Sing or play the interval of a fifth until you can do it from any pitch (this may take some time...keep at it).

3. On the first three lines and two spaces of the staff, draw whole notes on E, F, G, and A. Next you'll make a harmonic interval (one note directly over another) above each note you've already written. Write in the note an octave above the E, F, G, and the A. What are the names of these notes an octave above? Now, in between the note and the octave you've just written, write in the notes a perfect fifth above the bottom note. Now write in the note a major third above the bottom note. At each stage of the process, play and sing these intervals.

4. Using one of the tunes from Chapter 1 that you're memorizing or have memorized and identify all of the intervals in the melody. Do as many of them as you can handle. Sing them with the lyrics if the tune has lyrics.

CUTTING THE CHORDS

CHAPTER 5

CUTTING THE CHORDS

You can't always write a chord ugly enough to say what you want to say, so sometimes you have to rely on a giraffe filled with whipped cream.

~ Frank Zappa

In This Chapter

- Chord Generalities
- Chord Names, Numbers & Symbols
- Ear Training
- Chapter Review

Terms to Know

- Chord: 3 or more tones sounding at the same time.
- Diminished triad: 3-note chord with a root, minor 3rd, diminished 5th.
- Augmented triad: 3-note chord with a root, major 3rd, augmented 5th.
- cutting contest: a friendly rivalry between players. The best soloist "cuts" the others.

GENERAL CHORD INFO

The use of the word chord began, according to Webster's dictionary, around 1608, and is short for *accord*, which means to be in harmony, as in agreeing. It's a good word for a musical chord, because the notes in most chords tend to agree with each other. They sound good together.

The *Oxford Dictionary of Music* says a chord is *any simultaneous combination of notes, but usually of not fewer than three.* A chord can be played on one instrument like guitar or piano, or a chord can be played by many instruments at once, like a Dixieland trio, a big band, or a jazz septet. As long as there are three or more notes sounding simultaneously, it's a chord.

There are many types of chords, and many different chord symbols that tell you which notes to use in a chord. Just like with scales, there are major chords, minor chords, diminished chords and augmented chords. *The quality of a chord is determined by the intervals within the chord.*

There are other types of chords with more than three notes and several different treatments of chords, but for now let's keep it simple. We'll stick to the basics first, so you can get a handle on what chords are and how they work. While you're learning these chords, if you have access to a keyboard, you should play them to hear what they sound like.

NAMING CHORDS

A chord has two names. One is a letter name, the same as the root note of the chord. For example, a chord with a root of D is going to be some type of D chord. Pretty simple, right? The other is a number, a Roman numeral and this changes depending on the key signature (more on this later). Both the letter name and the Roman numeral are often seen with other symbols that show the chord qualities of major, minor, diminished, and augmented, all of which you'll learn in this chapter. Numbers are also used to show extensions, which we'll handle in the next chapter.

ROMAN NUMERALS

Each chord has a Roman numeral which corresponds to the degree of the scale on which the chord is built. Take a look at the example on the next page to see this. The upper case Roman numerals denote major triads, and lower case denotes minor triads. To show diminished and augmented chords, extra symbols are used. You'll see those soon, too.

LETTER NAMES

The letter name of the chords comes from the root (the bottom note) of the chord. Staff 5.1 below shows you what a root is. *If a chord is named with only a capital letter, this means the chord is major. A minor chord will have "min" written next to the letter.* Another method for showing minor is to use lower case letters, though it's more common to use the "min" next to the letter. In addition, the symbols for augmented and diminished are also used with the letter. We'll get to diminished and augmented chords soon.

When you say the notes in a chord, you're *spelling the chord.* For example, to spell the C chord I'd say, "C, E, G."

THE BASIC TRIAD

A basic triad consists of three notes stacked in a specific order, *a root (or bottom note and usually the letter name of the chord), a third, and a fifth.* As you'll see in the examples, each triad is built on all lines or all spaces. Notes in the triad get their name from their interval above the root.

Staff 5.1   Closely stacked triads in various positions on the staff.

TRIADS IN A MAJOR KEY

In the following example, you'll see a triad stacked on each degree of the C major scale. Triads stacked in this way will have a quality of either major, minor, or diminished. This is how chords in a particular scale are built.

Notice the little circle to the right of the vii. This symbol tells you the chord is a diminished chord. I'll show you why it's diminished coming up.

Staff 5.2   Triads built upon the degrees of the C major scale, with Roman numerals.

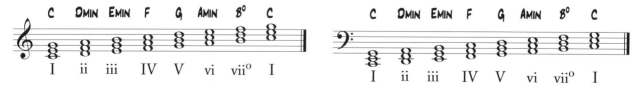

Major Triads

Major triads have a happy, bright sound quality. *A major triad consists of a note a major third above the root and another note a Perfect fifth above the root.*

In a major key, there are three naturally occurring major triads, those built upon the first, fourth, and fifth degrees of the scale, or the I, IV, and V chords.

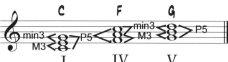

Minor Triads

Minor triads have a dark, sad, or melancholy sound quality. *A minor triad consists of a note a minor 3rd above the root and another note a Perfect 5th above the root.*

In a major key, there are three naturally occurring minor triads, those built upon the second, third, and sixth degrees of the major scale, or the ii, iii, and vi chords. Lots of options for the minor chord symbol: min, -, or just a lower-case "m." Find a cheat-sheet for these in the back of the book on the keyboard template.

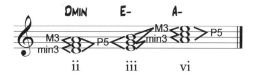

Diminished Triads

Diminished triads are less common than the major or minor triads and have a suspenseful sound quality. This is the chord you hear when the damsel in distress is tied to the railroad tracks by Dastardly Dan as an approaching train hoots in the near distance. *A diminished triad consists of a note a minor 3rd above the root and another note a diminished 5th above the root.*

In a major key, there is only one naturally occurring diminished triad, the one built on the seventh degree of the major scale.

Don't forget to put the little circle next to the lowercase Roman numeral. We'll get into more chord symbols in the next chapter.

Augmented Triads

There aren't any naturally occurring augmented triads in the key of C, or in any major key, so we'll have to throw in an accidental to get one. The augmented triad has a vaguely unsettling sound, and is usually the type of chord played just before the knife-wielding psycho jumps out from behind the couch and scares the cooties off your head. *An augmented triad consists of a note a major 3rd above the root and another note an augmented 5th above the root.*

Since there aren't any augmented triads occurring naturally in the key of C, I'll just make a couple up. The chord symbol for an augmented chord is a plus symbol (+), or the abbreviation "aug."

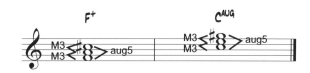

EAR TRAINING

1. The best thing you can do is sit down at a piano and play these, paying close attention with your ears. Start in the key of C (all white keys), and play the triads all the way up the scale. It's *really* easy so all you really have to do is just listen to the quality of each triad. You'll be doing double-duty by both building the chord and listening carefully. After you've got the key of C down, branch out to other keys. Build some triads starting on any note; try some black notes on the piano. Use the intervals to build the chords.

2. The next step is to use the sustain pedal (the one on the far right) so the chord rings out and as it does, play the notes on your instrument, then play the mode/scale associated with the chord. If you're playing any of the saxes, trumpet, clarinet or some other transposing instrument, make sure you're playing the right note. If you aren't sure, use your ears and find the exact same note you're playing on piano. Go to www.BasicJazzTheory.com if you need help with this.

3. If you've got a guitar and want to go that route, go for it! The only thing to be aware of playing the guitar is that the notes won't be "stacked" in the same way they are on piano; guitar isn't as intuitive of an instrument because it's notes are positioned both in a linear way (on each string), and a 6-dimensional way (across strings).

4. Listen to your recordings and try to identify chords you hear. This is much more difficult than it sounds, especially if you're listening to the good stuff, because those guys do all *sorts* of extra things to chords that make them tougher to identify: they flip the order of the notes (called *inversions*), they stack up more notes on top of the basic triad (called *extensions*), and they usually go by pretty fast. If you're listening to live music or video, it helps if you can see the musician's hands because you might be able to get some help there if you know what to look for.

IMPROVISE NOW

1. Play the root notes in a I-IV-V-I progression (in C that's: C-F-G-C), any rhythm. As you play that progression, another player improvises using the major scale of the key you're in. Stick with a groove for a while, then vary the rhythm, articulation, dynamics, and other aspects for a new groove.

2. Sit at a piano and improvise freely with chords. It doesn't matter what they're called. Play three or more notes at a time and just listen for the ones you like. Write the ones you like so you can use them in the next improvisation.

3. Play a chord from #1 on piano with the sustain pedal down (or play w/ a partner); improvise over the chord using the same scale/key. Alter articulations, sustain, movement, etc.

4. Form a trio, and one player is at the piano, the other two on an instrument. Stay in one particular key (C concert is great if you don't know much piano: all white keys). The person on piano plays chords in any order, of any type (try clusters of notes for fun). The other two listen and play along using the notes that goes with the key signature. If you play a transposing instrument (trumpet, sax, clarinet), make sure you're in the right key, or listen carefully.

Somethin' Else

Triads are the most basic chord form and it's important to know the difference between major, minor, diminished and augmented triads, so don't go on until you've got it.

In the next Chapter we'll add another note on top of the chord to make the triad a seventh chord, a type of chord extension. We'll also discuss other chord extensions. But first, the review.

Chapter Review

1. What is the definition of a chord?

2. What determines the quality of a chord?

3. How are chords named?

4. What are the parts of a triad?

5. Why are they called this?

6. How do you tell if a triad is major?

7. How do you tell if a triad is minor?

8. What are the intervals in a major triad?

9. What are the intervals in a minor triad?

10. What are the intervals in a diminished triad?

11. What are the intervals in an augmented triad?

12. What are the sound qualities of the different

1. Three or more notes played at the same time

2. The intervals within the chord

3. With a Roman numeral, a letter, and a quality of major, minor, diminished or augmented

4. Root, third, fifth

5. Root is the tonic of the chord; the third is a 3rd above the root; the fifth is a 5th above the root

6. Capital Roman numeral, a capital letter, or the intervals within the triad

7. Lowercase Roman numeral or letter; "min" next to the letter name; the triad's intervals

8. A note a major 3rd above the tonic and another a Perfect 5th above the tonic

9. A note a minor 3rd above the tonic and another a Perfect 5th above the tonic

10. A note a minor 3rd above the tonic and another a diminished 5th above the tonic

11. A note a major 3rd above the tonic and another an augmented 5th above the tonic

12. major = happy; minor=sad; diminished=suspenseful;

PRACTICAL USE

1. Have a friend play triads on a piano or guitar or other instrument. Identify the chords you hear. Take turns doing this so you also get a chance to build the chords. Try identifying an arpeggiated chord (this means chord tones are played one after the other instead of all at once).

2. Write out triads above the notes C, D, E, F and G. Sing *and* play these chords in an arpeggio (look this word up in the glossary if you don't know it) until you can hear each note in the chord easily. Play these notes as a chord on a piano or guitar. Identify which chords are major and which chords are minor. Identify by singing or playing the minor thirds and major thirds within these triads.

3. Write out four triads, all with D as their tonic. Make the first triad major, the second minor, the third diminished, and the fourth augmented. Play them on a piano. Memorize how they sound. Do the same thing starting on another note of your choice. Better yet, do it on all 12 notes.

CHAPTER 6

EXTENSION CHORDS

*But you can't extend, or go beyond any point
musically, without the basic fundamentals.*

~ Chico Hamilton

In This Chapter

- Chord Extensions
- 7th Chords
- 9th Chords
- 11th & 13th Chords
- Half-diminished Chords

Terms to Know

- extension: another chord tone stacked on top of the triad (7ths, 9ths, 11ths, 13ths)
- seventh chord: also known as the dominant, or the V chord. Usually leads to the tonic chord. Associated with the Mixolydian mode.
- dig: To know or understand completely. "Dig, man, there goes Mack the Knife!"

GENERAL CHORD EXTENSION INFO

A chord extension is a note that isn't in the triad. It's extra. Notes are added to triads to change the triad's flavor, their feel, and in many cases the extension changes how the chord is used.

Some notes added to triads are: 7ths, 9ths, 11ths, and 13ths. We haven't talked about intervals higher than octaves (called *compound intervals*), so now's the time.

If you look at the C scale in the example below, the 8th note is the same letter as the bottom note. Therefore, the 9th note is the same letter as the 2nd note of the scale, only it's an octave higher. The 11th is like a 4th, but an octave higher; the 13th is like a 6th, but an octave higher.

Staff 6.1   The C scale extended two octaves. Interval is counted from the lowest note. This example starts on C but it could be any note. The lowest note is always 1.

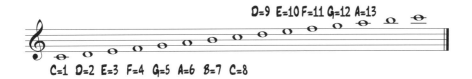

Chords with extensions are written with the number of the extension above and to the right of the chord letter, like so: F^{b13}, A^7, G^9, $C^{\#11}$, F^{13}, D^{Maj7}, and so on. Extensions can also be used with Roman numerals, like V^7, IV^9, etc.

The number tells you which note you're adding to the triad. The number represents the interval from the root of the chord to the extension. For example, a chord symbol with a 7 in it means that you're adding a note a 7th above the root of the chord.

Chord Symbol	Meaning
min, -	minor
M, Maj, △	major
O	diminished
Ø	half-diminished
aug, +	scale tone above root is raised 1/2 step

An extension can be altered a half step up or down to give yet another type of chord. In the examples I gave you above, there was an F chord with a b13, a C chord with a #11, and a D chord with a Maj7. In these cases you would lower the 13th a half step, raise the 11th a half step or use a Major 7th above the root, respectively. On to some specifics.

SEVENTH CHORDS

Seventh chords are an important type of chord in Western music as well as music from other traditions. They're essential to most chord progressions, and give progressions the quality our ears are used to hearing. We'll get into specifics of chord progressions in *BJT volume 2*.

The seventh chords have a property that other extensions don't have. When you see *a seven next to a chord symbol, it's always a minor 7th above the root*. If you want a Major seventh above the root, you have to specify it in the extension by putting an "M" or a "Maj" or a small triangle "△" in front of the extension number (the triangle implies the Maj 7).

As you can see in the above examples, the quality of the chord itself is written in larger letters next to the letter of the chord (except for Major chords which are just the letter), and any alterations to the 7th are written in small letters before the 7.

THE DOMINANT SEVENTH CHORD

There is a special kind of seventh chord which appears in a huge majority of chord progressions and it's called the *dominant seventh chord*. The dominant seventh chord symbol looks like this: V^7. When you see something like C^7, Db^7, E^7, etc., it's a dominant seventh only if the chord is built on the 5th degree of scale/key you're playing in.

Because you know how Roman numerals are used, you know that the above symbol means that the chord is built on the 5th degree of the scale and it's got a minor seventh in it. I didn't tell you each scale degree had a name when we went over scales because you had enough to worry about without me giving you more information than was necessary, but now it's necessary.

Each scale degree has a name, and it just so happens that the name of the 5th degree of the scale is "dominant." That's why a chord built on the 5th degree of the scale is called a dominant chord, and one with a seventh is called a dominant seventh chord.

For now we'll focus on the dominant seventh chord. It's important because it pulls our ears back toward the tonic chord, or the I chord. More on that when we talk about chord progressions in *Basic Jazz Theory vol. 2*.

Scale Degree	Scale Degree Name	Associated Chord's Roman Numeral.
1	Tonic	I
2	Supertonic	ii
3	Mediant	iii
4	Subdominant	IV
5	Dominant	V
6	Submediant	vi
7	Leading Tone	vii

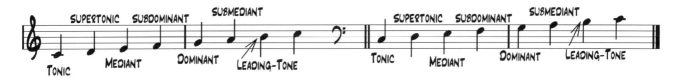

Staff 6.2   Dominant seventh chords in the keys of C, G, Bb, and F. Each chord is built on the key's 5th degree.

Notice that each measure uses a different key signature. When you build a chord on the 5th degree of the scale in any Major key, the seventh of V^7 will automatically be a minor seventh because of the key signature.

Ninth Chords

Ninth chords have 5 chord tones: Root, third, fifth, seventh, and ninth.

As before, the quality of the chord is written in larger letters next to the chord letter, and the extensions are written with smaller letters and numbers above and to the right. If all you see is a "9", the 7 is implied. However, if you want a *Major* 7th in there (remember that unless indicated, the 7th is always minor), you must specify it, as in the $G^{M7, 9}$ and the $Ab^{M7\ 9}$ below. You usually won't see a comma (,) in the chord name, as in the examples below, but you might.

Staff 6.3   Some ninth chords.

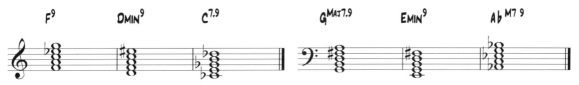

Extending Further

Eleventh and Thirteenth Chords

The process for these chords is very similar to what you already know. An eleventh chord will have a root, third, fifth, seventh, ninth and eleventh.

A thirteenth chord will have a root, third, fifth, seventh, ninth, eleventh, and thirteenth. For extensions in C, sit at a piano and simply play *every other note*: three notes is a triad, four notes is a seventh chord, five notes is a ninth chord, and six notes is a thirteenth chord.

The Half Diminished Chord

If we build a 7th chord on the 7th degree of the major scale (we'll stay in the key of C to avoid accidentals), you get a chord that's called half-diminished. That's a diminished triad (stacked minor thirds, remember?), with a minor 7th above the root. Here's an example:

Half Diminished Chord Symbols

In a longer form, the following chord would be notated $Bmin^{7b5}$ or $B\text{-}^{7b5}$, but a shorter version which gives the same information is $B^{\emptyset}$.

Staff 6.4   The $Bmin^{7b5}$, or the $B\text{-}^{7b5}$, or the B half-diminished chord, or as it's usually notated: $B^{\emptyset}$.

Are all these symbols confusing? Without a doubt. The reason for the shortening of the symbols is that when jazz musicians are reading through chord changes while they improvise, it's more difficult and time-consuming to read $Cmin^{7b5}$, which has 5 "bits" of information, than it is to read $C^{\emptyset}$, which has only two "bits" of information. The less bits, the quicker you can read.

Ear Training

1. As with most ear-training, these sounds are best explored at a piano keyboard. Build a major triad in any key (stick with C, the white keys, if you're still learning). Add the major 7th and listen carefully. Sing all chord tones with the piano and then on your own! Change the extension to a minor 7th and *listen* to the difference. Sing the tones! Go back and forth between the two types of chord. Repeat in another key. Have a partner play one or the other and see (hear, actually) if you can identify the difference. Sing these when you're away from the piano. Change where you play the chord tones on the piano. Use the same notes in different positions. Can you still hear and identify the chord quality?

2. It's much better to sit at a piano and do these, but there are many sources for ear-training free online. Run a search of your own because you might find a new and better version than the following. But, you can try these:

- www.musictheory.net/exercises: Excellent and highly customizable: practice exactly what you want. Intervals, scales, and chords. Digitized piano sound isn't all that great, but it's free, so no whining.
- www.good-ear.com: Simple, easy to navigate, jazz options. Digitized sounds are low quality.
- www.trainear.com: A downloadable free program, so you can practice without an Internet connection.

IMPROVISE NOW

1. Double up on your practice. Play a chord you're trying to learn (dominant 7th chords are a great place to start) and keep the sustain pedal of the piano down so the sound resonates. Have a partner play the chord if you can and take turns. Improvise over the chord using the mode associated with it. For example, the F7 is associated with the F Mixolydian mode. Use repetition, sequences, rhythmic play, and don't forget to use space, or silence, too. If you play a transposing instrument like trumpet, clarinet, or all saxes, make sure you're playing the correct notes!

2. Do #1 with another person and take turns at the piano.

SOMETHIN' ELSE

This chapter should allow you to understand and spell most chords you'll come across. Again, the concepts you're now learning are more complex than previous ones and they may take some time before you own them (meaning you can hear them), so keep at it. All the chords in this chapter have been in root position, the most basic form of a chord. Know that chords often to not appear in this neat arrangement. The notes can be in any position at all. Chords in other than root position are called inversions.

CHAPTER REVIEW

1. What is a chord extension?

2. How are chord extensions notated?

3. What is a compound interval?

4. When you see a ^{7} to the right of a chord letter, what kind of a 7th is it?

5. How would you indicate a Major 7 above the root?

6. What's another name for the V^{7}chord?

1. A note that doesn't appear in the basic triad

2. A number equal to the note's interval above the root. Also with a symbol showing quality

3. An interval greater than an octave.

4. A minor 7th above the root.

5. With a a small triangle, a capital "M", or a small "Maj" before the 7.

6. Dominant seventh chord

7. Why are V^7 chords so important?

7. They draw the ear to the tonic (I) chord, and appear in nearly all chord progressions

8. Spell the V^7 chord in the key of G.

8. D,F#,A,C

9. Which chord tones are in a 9th chord?

9. Root, 3rd, 5th, 7th, 9th

10. Which chord tones are in an 11th chord?

10. Root, 3rd, 5th, 7th, 9th, 11th

11. Spell a C^7 chord.

11. C, E, G, Bb

12. Spell a D^9 chord.

12. D, F#, A, C, E

PRACTICAL USE

1. Write out the triads above C, A, B-flat, and A-flat. Put the chord name underneath (don't forget Major/minor distinctions). Place the seventh in each of the chords and alter the chord symbol as necessary to make it correct. Place the ninth in each chord and again correct the chord symbol.

2. Sing and play a Major triad. Any starting note will do but make it in a comfortable range. As you sing one note of the chord, try to hear the others simultaneously. Hear a chord tone other than the one you're singing, then switch to sing the chord tone you "heard" silently. Once the Major triad is in your ear, add the seventh (both major and minor) until you can sing or play both sevenths easily. Do the same with the ninth chord.

3. Spend some time messing around with triads and extensions on the piano. It's fun and will help your understanding immensely.

Chapter 7

Pentatonic and Blues Scales

Blues is easy to play, but hard to feel.

~ Jimi Hendrix

In This Chapter

- Major Pentatonic Scale
- Minor Pentatonic Scale
- Basic Blues Scale
- Other Blues Scales
- Blues Form

Terms to Know

- diatonic scale: scales with notes that progress stepwise with no leaps.
- gapped scale: scales that have leaps larger than a 2nd.
- bent: a note changed slightly up or down to be more expressive.
- clam: a wrong note or mistake.
- cans: headphones (not earbuds).

Blues: the Bones of Jazz

Jazz without the blues would be like cubism without Picasso, or gumbo without roux. It simply wouldn't happen. The blues style has influenced *many* types of music, including jazz. American anthologist of black culture James Weldon Johnson said, "It is from the blues that all that may be called American music derives its distinct characteristics." You've been listening to echoes of the blues all your life.

Because the blues are so important, I almost made this the first chapter, but then realized that in order to really *get* this scale, it would help to know other things first, like major scales and intervals, and one other thing. Before we get to the blues scale, we're going to talk briefly about another kind of scale, the pentatonic scale, because these will also help you understand (and play/hear) the blues scale.

First let's check out two other types of gapped scales, the major and minor pentatonic scales. Both of these—especially the minor pentatonic—are closely related to the blues scale.

General Pentatonic Scale Info

I'm sure you've already guess that there are 5 notes in the pentatonic scale, just as there are 5 sides to a pentagon. This is a type of *gapped scale*, which means that its notes don't proceed stepwise, or *diatonically*; there's a leap in there. Both of these scales avoid the use of the half step that we saw in major scale and related modes. The lack of half steps gives pentatonic scales an open quality. These series of pitches have been used in many Asian musics, and you'll probably be able to hear that when you play them.

Pentatonic scales are closely related to the major scale. All the notes you'll find in both the major and minor pentatonic scale are also in the major scale. But wait, there's more! The major and minor pentatonic scales share the *exact same notes*, you just start in different places. It's the same principle we explored with modes. Remember that the mode built on the 6th degree of the major scale is known as the natural minor scale, right? That same principle will help us build a minor pentatonic off the 6th degree. But let's start with the major pentatonic.

THE MAJOR PENTATONIC SCALE

What do you get if you take the half steps out of a major scale? The answer is a major pentatonic scale. So, the half steps in a major scale come between degrees 3-4 (E to F) and between degrees 7-8 (B to C). If we take out the 4th (F) and 7th (B) degrees of the scale, we're left with 1, 2, 3, 5, 6, right? Right. That's the major pentatonic. Here's an example in C:

Staff 7.1   The major pentatonic scale ascending and descending. Play it on your instrument, the piano, and *sing it*!

THE MINOR PENTATONIC SCALE

Remember when you played the Aeolian mode, the one that starts on the 6th degree of the major scale? So in our example, the 6th degree of the C major scale is A. It's also called the natural minor scale and it's the basis for the minor pentatonic scale. It's also *very* similar to the blues scale which you'll see in a few more paragraphs.

Just as with the major pentatonic, there are no half steps in the minor pentatonic scale either. Where do the half steps lie in the natural minor scale? Think about it for a second and see if you can figure it out. I'll wait.... Okay, you should've come up with those natural half steps between 2-3 (the B to the C) and 5-6 (the E to the F). So if we take those notes, the B and the F, just like we did with the major pentatonic, we're left with 1, 3, 4, 5, 7, right? Right. Here's how the minor pentatonic looks. Notice that it uses the *exact same notes* as the major pentatonic above. These scales are related, and this is why it's sometimes called the relative minor. Each key signature has a relative minor that shares the same key signature, or notes. In this case, the relative minor of C Major is A minor. Make sense?

Staff 7.2   The A minor pentatonic scale. Play it. Sing it. Own it.

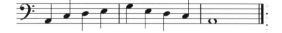

As with all other scales, work these through all key signatures. Coming up, we'll add just one more note to the minor pentatonic to get the blues scale. Read on....

General Blues Scale Info

Most people like blues scales. They sound cool, are fun to play and easy to learn. They also come in handy if you're improvising in blues, rock and roll, country, jazz, and many other styles of music. Like all the other scales, the blues scale can be made by altering notes of the major scale. These altered notes are called *blue* notes, and the practice came to us from Africans who were brought to this country as slaves. A blue note was originally a bending of the pitch with the voice.

Some think the use of "the blues" as a term for feeling down came from a Native American tribe in the south who would cover their bodies with a blue dye when they were in mourning. Slaves in the area saw the practice and invented the term "feeling blue." Maybe it's just legend, but it's a story I like because it combines the artistry of two important peoples in US history, people who have made invaluable contributions to modern culture despite—or perhaps because of—their oppression. That's powerful stuff.

Every blues scale is related to a major scale, and it's the same relationship as the minor pentatonic, which is to say it's built on the 6th degree of the major scale. Let's say you're sitting in with some Country musicians and by noodling around, you discover that they're playing in the key of C major. Because you're a savvy musician, you know that if you use the blues scale that starts on the 6th degree of that scale, it'll sound great and go well with what the other musicians are playing. You can think of it as a Maj 6th above the key or a minor third below. Same note name.

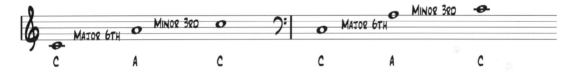

Standard Blues Scale

The *standard blues scale* is also called the minor blues scale, or more commonly, simply the blues scale. Given its relation to the minor pentatonic, this shouldn't come as a surprise to you. Because this scale has one more note than a pentatonic scale, it's a hexatonic scale, meaning it has 6 notes. We'll use the A blues scale so you can see its similarity to the A minor pentatonic. Can you spot the extra note?

Staff 7.3   The A blues scale. Notice the Eb? That's the extra note and in this case it's called a flat 5. Do you see why?

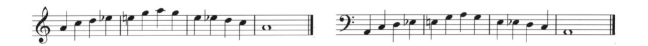

I've used what is called a *flat 5* for the blue note, meaning I've lowered the perfect 5th by a half step. Some think the blue note should be a sharp 4 (in our example a D#) instead of a flat 5 (the E♭ in our example), but the way I hear this, that blue note is a fifth that is *bent* downward. The sound leads into the 5, and so that's why I've chosen to show it as a flat 5 instead of a sharp 4. you might see it either way in written music, but don't let that confuse you. It sounds the same, and that's the important thing.

Below are three ways to create a blues scale: one version builds the scale from the minor pentatonic and the other uses the major scale as a reference. You might find one method easier than another.

Recipe #1 for Any Standard Blues Scale (Minor Pentatonic method)

1 Take one minor pentatonic scale of your choice (it's good to know which major scale it's related to so that you're ready when you have to jam in a major key. Hint: the 2nd note of the blues scale is the name of the major key/scale to which it's related. For example, the 2nd note of the A blues scale is a C.).

2 Add the note that goes between the 2nd and 3rd notes of the minor pentatonic. This means you have 3 chromatic notes in the scale. If you look at our example, you'll see that D-E♭-E are the 3 chromatic notes in the A blues scale.

3 Learn to play the scale on a piano keyboard.

4 Sing the scale at the piano so you know you're getting it right. Sing it without the piano.

5 Turn over lightly in your brain and under your fingers until memorized.

6 Repeat from step one with a new scale until all 12 are memorized.

Recipe #2 for Any Standard Blues Scale (Major scale method)

1 Take one major scale of your choice

2 Use the tonic of the major scale as the first note of the blues scale.

3 Lower the third degree of the major scale a half step to get the second degree of the blues scale.

4 Use the P4 of the major scale as the 3rd note of the blues scale.

5 Lower the P5 of the major scale by a half step to get the 4th note of the blues scale.

6 Use the P5 of the major scale for the 5th note of the blues scale. This will involve using an accidental (a natural or a sharp) to cancel the one you used to lower the 4th note of the blues scale.

7 Take the seventh degree of the Major scale and lower it a half step for the 6th degree of the blues scale.

8 Use the P8 for the seventh note of the blues scale.

9 Knead in your brain and under your fingers until fully mixed and memorized.

10 Repeat from step one with a new scale until all 12 are memorized.

Use Your Blues

Hendrix wasn't lying when he said, "Playing the blues is easy, but feeling the blues is hard." It takes a *lot* of experience to feel the blues like Big Bill Broonzy, or Muddy Waters, or BB King or Clifford Brown, or Oscar Peterson. But the only way to get there is to start right now.

The blues is a great example of how written music simply can't convey the spirit of a sound. The blues is inflection, and feeling. The blues has notes that are bent up, bent down, and twisted in ways that simply can't be notated. When I play I'll use half-valve techniques on the trumpet to bend notes up or down. All instruments except piano can bend notes in this way. Find out what those techniques are for your instrument. Listen to Billy Holliday or Ella Fitzgerald bend notes to hear a master do it.

On brass instruments like trumpet and trombone, a plunger helps shape the notes even more; it can sound just like a voice. Listen to Tricky Sam Nanton, trombonist in the Duke Ellington band, or Wycliff Gordon, another trombonist who uses the plunger and plays in a bluesy style. On trumpet you can check out Cootie Williams or Bubber Miley (also with the Ellington band), Wynton Marsalis (especially *The Seductress*—not a blues it's got a haunting vocal quality. Find it at: http://yhoo.it/beCQyf), or run a YouTube search on Ryan Kisor playing *Concerto for Cootie* and you'll hear what I mean. Guitar players bend strings all over the place to shape notes, too. Listen to BB King or Stevie Ray Vaughn or Lightning Hopkins to hear the blues in action.

Ear Training

1. Sing a blues scale. Better yet, sing along with a blues recording that has vocals.

2. Find a bunch of recordings of the blues and compare them. Some blues progressions are very simple, some much more complex. As one example of a complex blues, listen to *Blues for Alice* by Charlie Parker, or *Goodbye Pork Pie Hat*, Thelonius Monk's tribute to Lester Young who often wore a pork pie hat. These are *not* simple blues, but use the same 12 bars and similar rules.

Improvise Now

1. Mess around with the A blues scale. Improvise freely with no rhythm or chords at all. Anything goes. Try bending notes, using half valves (if you play a valve instrument), alternate fingerings, glissando (especially you trombone players). Keep it simple.

2. Add rhythm and repeat #1. It can be just a metronome, or maybe a drum set with brushes, or a tumbao on conga, or anything. Lots of rhythms available online for free. Continue to play with the scale freely, but stay with the rhythmic pulse. This works best with a live person!

3. Repeat #1 and #2 but with a partner, trios, quartets, quintets, and if you're brave, even larger groups, like a whole band.

4. Find a blues tune by any of the artists mentioned above. Find the key signature by ear and improvise along using the blues scale that fits the key.

Somethin' Else

These 7 chapters have given you a LOT to practice and a lot to wrap your head and your ears around, so give it some time to soak in. In the appendix to this book you'll find all the major, natural minor, and blues scales to practice. Don't neglect just playing by ear! Try to figure out tunes and key signatures without referring to written music. It can be frustrating to learn like this, but that frustration is the sign that you're learning, that you're pushing yourself, that you're growing myelin around your neurons. For a good book on the subject, check out *The Talent Code*, by Dan Coyle.

Chapter Review

1. How do you find the major scale associated with the blues scale?

2. What is a gapped scale?

3. How do you build a blues scale from the minor pentatonic?

4. What is a blue note?

5. How do you find the blues scale associated with the major scale?

6. Have you practiced your scales today?

1. The second note of the blues scale is the first note of the major scale associated with the blues scale.

2. A scale with intervals of more than a second between some notes of the scale.

3. Add the note between the 2nd and 3rd note of the minor pentatonic.

4. An altered note (usu. bent lower).

5. The sixth note of the major scale is the starting note for the blues scale. Think relative minor.

Practical Use

1. When you play/practice a major scale for the next month (or longer), play the associated blues scale, too.

2. Write out the following blues scales below: E, F, G, and Bb. Play them to see/hear if they sound right. Check your work by looking at the scales in the appendix of this book. Play them.

3. Find any blues recording and figure out what key they're in. Improvise along. Hint: most blues don't involve lots of sharps or flats; try A, E, D, and G blues first. Use your ears.

CHAPTER 8

LISTEN & LEARN

*To listen well, is as powerful a means of influence as to
talk well, and is as essential to all true conversation.*

~ Chinese proverb

In This Chapter

- Why Listen?
- Listening tips
- Basic Jazz Styles
- Album Lists

Terms to Know

- blow: to improvise. Also to play any instrument.
- axe: your instrument.
- bag: a person's particular "thing." Cutting contests just ain't my *bag*.
- tubs: another name for drums.
- skins: another name for drums.

WHY LISTEN?

Listening to music requires you only to have a pair of working ears (with a brain connected). You don't need the special skills required to actually *play* jazz, you only need the skills required to play your radio, CD player, MP3 player, cassette player, or turntable. Or for those of you retro-rebels, your 8-track, reel-to-reel machines, or Victrolas.

Recordings are the easiest and least expensive way to experience great music made by the Masters. However, recordings aren't the *best* way to experience jazz. The best way is to hear jazz *live*, created in the same room with you. There is no other experience like it and after your first good experience, you'll be hooked. The real-time exchange of improvised ideas is truly amazing. But wait, there's more!

When we watch someone do something the *exact same neurons* that are required to perform the task we see fire in our *own* brain! And the more we've practiced that which we watch, the more of the correct neurons fire while we watch. It's not clear whether this counts as practice, but it does explain to me why listening and watching live musicians gives you a sense that it's possible for you to do it, too. That's priceless. Chances are that you can probably talk to these musicians, too, or ask to take a lesson. Goethe said, "Be bold. The mighty forces will come to your aid."

Listening is far and away the *very* best thing you can do for your jazz playing and your musicianship skills. There is no substitute for it. Listening to music is food for your own music. If you don't listen to other players, your road to jazz mastery will be short and lonely. That would be sad. Stuff your ears with wonder!

WHERE TO LISTEN ONLINE

There is *so* much jazz out there for you to hear—over 100 years' worth—that it can be intimidating to even start, and it can be a little confusing to the uninitiated.

For recorded jazz, as of this writing, there are four fantastic online resources at which you can listen for free and explore what jazz has to offer. I'm *still* discovering great albums and tunes I hadn't heard of before. Enter any of the tunes, albums or artists listed below at the following sites:

* www.accujazz.com: *Very* well organized jazz collection. Choose jazz by decade, instrument, style, musician, region, and 14 (yes, 14!) other categories. This is the best place to start if you have no idea what you like or who to listen to, or even if you do. Go there now!

* www.pandora.com: You probably already know this one. Choose a musician, a song, an album, or a style. You'll also get other musicians/songs that are similar to the choice you made and your own custom radio station is there for you to hear. A great resource that requires a bit of knowledge from you, but totally worth it. In fact, right now, I'm listening to a track by trumpeter Don Byrd I've never heard before, and it's great! I think I'll click the "buy" button....

* www.youtube.com: Use the two sites above to find the names of jazz musicians who have videos on YouTube. You'd be surprised how far back you can go with video. Some have posted songs with slide-show image montages which can be fun to watch. On some the quality isn't so hot, but to actually watch Louis Armstrong or Sonny Rollins or Ella Fitzgerald is pretty amazing. Almost as good as live music.

* www.shufflr.fm: Explore *many* different styles through others' blogs. The link to jazz is on page 2.

A FAST AND LOOSE JAZZ STYLES CHEAT SHEET

When I was in my early teens in Sitka, a small town on an island in Southeast Alaska, I wanted to find out what this whole *jazz* thing was about. This was long before the Internet. I had heard of Miles Davis and figured I should get one of his albums and chose *Bitches Brew*. Those of you who know this album are probably laughing. It's a successful jazz fusion album that was *way* out there to my poor untrained ears. My first reaction was, *This is jazz? I don't think I like jazz.....* Fortunately, I persisted in my search and now that I have a *lot* more listening experience, I enjoy the album and have tasted most of the other flavors jazz has to offer.

I hope to help you avoid any misunderstandings like I experienced back then through these lists. I'd also like to challenge you to open up your ears and your mind to different sounds and different styles of jazz. Something that you may react to unfavorably on first hearing might become an old and dear friend if you keep trying to understand it. Often we dislike what we don't understand. Here's a rough overview of the most common jazz styles:

JAZZ STYLE	BRIEF DESCRIPTION
Old-School/Dixieland (1900-1930+)	small groups, group improvisation, improvised harmony (2nd line), often straight-eighth note feel, poor sound quality due to nascent recording technology.
Big Band (1930-1950+)	large (20+) bands, sax, 'bone, & trumpet sections, full rhythm section (p, b, g, d)
Bebop (1940-1960+)	blistering speed, complex harmony, some believe it's the pinnacle of jazz skill
Modal Jazz (1959-1970+)	less complex harmony, melodic focus, a reaction to the complexity of 'bop

Jazz Style	Brief Description
Gypsy Jazz (1930-)	2 rhythm guitars, 1 lead gtr, bass, guitar virtuosity, often no drums, sometimes violin, accordion or wind instruments.
Latin Jazz (1945-)	incorporates Afro-Cuban music: rhythms, instruments, grooves, etc. Fun!
Jazz Fusion (1968-1990+)	incorporates elements of other music like rock, funk, etc. Led by Miles Davis
Smooth Jazz (1975-)	R&B/Soul influenced, slow grooves (90-105 BPM), highly processed sound, commercial. Often dismissed and/or reviled by "serious" jazzers.

Listening Suggestions

I'm reluctant to suggest *anything*, because I'll inevitably leave something or someone out and I'll be sure to hear about it, but I'm going to do it anyway, because there are some jazz albums and jazz musicians that *everyone* should listen to, or at least know about.

The lists below are only a miniscule selection of some of my favorite albums, those that I think are most approachable or the most important. I've broken them down into several categories and except for the first, each category contains 5 albums (often boxed sets). This will help keep things simple until you start to branch out on your own into the deeper jazz waters. Use these lists to get a feel for what's out there and what you like. Except for the first, the categories are roughly chronological, with the last few categories separated by instrument and drawn from all of the genres listed and then some. Artists are listed with their instrument:

piano (p), bass (b), drums (d), soprano sax (ss), alto sax (as), tenor sax (ts), baritone sax (bs), trumpet (t), trombone (tb), guitar (g), vocalist (v).

You can find all these albums available for purchase as CD or mp3 and many other important resources including transcribed solos and fake books containing most of these tunes at www.BasicJazzTheory.com.

10 Excellent Jazz Albums

Album Title	Artist(s)
A Night at Birdland, vol. 1	Blakey(d), Brown(t), Silver (p), Russel (b), Donaldson (as),
Saxophone Colossus	Rollins(ts), Flanagan(p), Watkins(b), Roach(d)
Somethin' Else	Adderly (as), Davis (t), H. Jones(p), S. Jones(b), Blakey(d)
Open Sesame	Hubbard (t), Brooks (ts), Tyner (p), S. Jones (b), Jarvis (d)
Bobby Broom Plays for Monk	Bobby Broom (g), Dennis Carroll (b), Kobie Watkins (d)
Diz & Getz	Gillespie (t), Getz (ts), Ellis (g), Peterson (p), R. Brown(b), Roach(d)
Blue Train	Coltrane (ts), Chambers (b), Drew (p), Fuller (t), P.J. Jones (d), Morgan (t)
The Great Ladies Sing Gershwin	Ella Fitzgerald (v), Sarah Vaughan (v), Nina Simone (v), Shirley Horn (v), Dinah Washington (v), Betty Carter (v), various rhythm section players
A Tribute to Miles	Roney (t), Shorter (as), Hancock (p), Carter (b), Williams (d)
Verve Jazz Masters 44	Clifford Brown (t), Max Roach (d), various others

5 Essential Old-School Jazz Albums

Album Title	Artist(s)
Hot Fives & Sevens (2 discs)	Louis Armstrong, (t), various others
Singin' the Blues 1	Bix Beiderbecke (cornet), various others
King Oliver's Creole Jazz Band: The Complete Set	Joe "King" Oliver (cornet), various others
Jelly Roll Morton: 1926-1930 (5 discs)	Jelly Roll Morton (p), various others
The Original James P. Johnson	James P. Johnson (p), various others

5 Essential Big Band Jazz Albums

Album Title	Band Leader (soloists)
Duke Ellington Masterpieces 1926-1949	Duke Ellington (p), (Cootie, Hodges, Tricky Sam, Bubber, et al)
The Complete Decca Recordings (3 discs)	Count Basie (p), (L. Young, Sweets Edison, H. Evans, et al)
Self Portrait (5 discs)	Artie Shaw (cl), various others
Consummation	Thad Jones (flugel), Mel Lewis (d), various others
Sing Sing Sing	Benny Goodman (Gene Krupa, Harry James, various others)

5 Essential Bebop/Hard Bop Jazz Albums

Album Title	Artist(s)
Jazz at Massey Hall	Parker (as), Gillespie (t), Mingus (b), Powell (p), Roach (d)
Tenor Madness	Rollins (ts), Garland (p), Chambers (b), PJ Jones (d), Coltrane (ts-1trk)
The Best of Lee Morgan	Lee Morgan, various others
The Best of Charlie Parker	Charlie Parker (as), various others
Amazing Bud Powell, vol. 1	Bud Powell (p), Duvivier/Russel (b), Taylor/Roach (d)

5 Essential Modal Jazz (influenced) Albums

Album Title	Artist(s)
Kind of Blue	Miles Davis (t), Adderly (as), Evans/Kelly (p), Chambers (b), Cobb (d)
Live! At the Village Vanguard (1961)	John Coltrane (ss, ts), Tyner (p), Workman/Garrison (b), Jones/Haynes (d), Dolphy (b. clar), Bushell (oboe, cntrabssn), Malik (oud)
Speak No Evil	Wayne Shorter (as), Hancock (p), Carter, (b), Jones (d)
Maiden Voyage	Herbie Hancock (p), Hubbard (t), Coleman (ts), Carter (b), Williams (d)
A Love Supreme	John Coltrane (ss, ts), Tyner (p), Garrison (b), Jones (d)

5 Essential Gypsy Jazz Albums

Album Title	Artist(s)
Best of Django Reinhardt	Django Reinhardt (g), Stephane Grapelli (viol.), various others
Gypsy Project	Bireli Lagrene (g), Niculescu (viol.), Galliano (accor.), various others
Djangologists	Stochello and Jimmy Rosenbergs(g), B. Lagrene, others
Hot Club Records: The Best Of	various: Grapelli (viol), Rosenbergs, Debarre, Lagrene, many others
Les Nuits Manouche: The Best...	various: Reinhardt, Schmitt, Niculescu, various others

5 Essential Latin Jazz Albums

Album Title	Artist(s)
Bossa Nova (aka Getz/Gilberto)	Stan Getz (ts), Jao Gilberto, Astrid Gilberto, various others
King of Kings: The Very Best	Tito Puente (timbales, marimba, etc.), various others
Dizzy's Diamonds, disc 3	Dizzy Gillespie (t), many others
Latin Soul	Poncho Sanchez (v, cnga, perc.), various others
Stone Flower	Jobim (p, g,), Carter (b), Moreira (perc), Green (tb), various others

5 Essential Piano Jazz Albums

Album Title	Artist(s)
Saturday Night at the Blue Note	Oscar Peterson (p), Ellis (g), Brown (b), Durham (d)
Sahara	McCoy Tyner (p, koto, perc), Fortune (as,ss,flt), Hill (b), Mouzon (d)
Koln Concert	Keith Jarrett (p)
Money Jungle	Duke Ellington (p), Charles Mingus (b), Max Roach (d)
Portrait in Jazz	Bill Evans (p), Lafaro (b), Motian (d),

5 Essential Jazz Trumpet Albums

Album Title	Artist(s)
Clifford Brown & Max Roach	Clifford Brown (t), Max Roach (d), R Powell (p), Morrow (b), Land (ts)
The Artist Selects	Freddie Hubbard (t), various others
Night in Tunisia: Best of Dizzy	Dizzy Gillespie (t), various others
Afro Cuban	Kenny Dorham (t), Blakey (d), "Patato" (cnga), Johnson (tb), others
Milestones	Miles Davis (t), Adderly (as), Coltrane (ts), Garland (p), Chambers (b), PJ Jones (d)

5 Essential Jazz Saxophone Albums

Album Title	Artist(s)
Saxophone Colossus	Sonny Rollins (ts), Flanagan (p), Watkins (b), Roach (d)
A Love Supreme	John Coltrane (ss, ts), Tyner (p), Garrison (b), Jones (d)
The Essential Charlie Parker	Charlie Parker, various others
Lester Young with The O. P. Trio	Lester Young (ts), Oscar Peterson (p), Kessel (g), Brown (b), Heard (d)
Body and Soul	Coleman Hawkins (ts), various others

5 Essential Jazz Guitar Albums

Album Title	Artist(s)
Smokin' at the Half Note	Wes Montgomery (g), Kelly (p), Chambers (b), Cobb (d)
Midnight Blue	Kenny Burrell (g), Turrentine (ts), Holley (b), Barretto (cga), English (d)
Best Of	Joe Pass (g), various others
Gravy Waltz	Herb Ellis (g), various others
Charlie Christian: Genius of the Electric Guitar	Charlie Christian (g), Cootie Williams (t), Lester Young (ts), Gene Krupa (d), Benny Goodman (cl), Count Basie (p), many others

Improvise Now

These recordings are some of the very best teachers you'll have. After you've found a few tunes that speak to you, that you really like, and that you've listened to enough to have a good idea how they go, grab your horn and start playing along! At first this will probably be difficult and a little frustrating (especially with a bebop tune!), but stick with it. It can take quite a while. In *BJT vol 3* I'll introduce you to some tools to make this easier. For now, just have at it! You can also find many transcriptions of these tunes at BasicJazzTheory.com.

Only the Beginning

These short lists barely scratch the surface; I've only included tunes or artists that stand out, are classics of the form, or are easy to listen to. In *Basic Jazz Theory volume 2* and *volume 3*, I'll give you even more listening suggestions, including masters burning bright today. Seek out your own favorites using the tools in this chapter! You won't regret it.

CODICIL

INDEX   PIANO KEYBOARD

SCALES   GUITAR FINGERBOARD

FIND MORE RESOURCES AT:

www.BasicJazzTheory.com

Basic Jazz Theory
Volume 2

The journey continues in volume 2 using the same friendly format of chapter quizzes, practical use, and ear training suggestions. Here's what you'll find in *Basic Jazz Theory, volume 2*:

* Chord progressions: V-I, ii-V-I, iii-vi-ii-V-I, etc.
* Form: AABA, Blues,
* Rhythm changes and variations
* Substitutions
* The Circle of Fifths and How to Use It
* The Practice of Jazz Practice
* More Listening Suggestions
* Quizzes
* Practical Use Exercises
* Ear Training Exercises
* Other Practice Resources

Available January, 2011

Other Books from Jonathan Harnum
Visit us on the web: www.sol-ut.com

Basic Music Theory: How to Read, Write, and Understand Written Music

Don't know how to read music at all? This book will help you out with note names, clefs, key signatures, time signatures, musical terms, basic chords and progressions, the guitar fingerboard and piano keyboard, and more. Similar format to the *BJT* series with quizzes and practical use exercises. Also interludes on practice, conducting, and musical terms.

Sound the Trumpet: How to Blow Your Own Horn

Contains everything you need to know including all the basics: tone production, fingering, tonguing, the breath, and more, as well as information not in any other trumpet method book: discographies, how to clean the horn, practice tips, scales, and more. Also has useful material in the back: practice tracking forms, scales, piano keyboard, book index.

I N D E X

Scales Checklist

Major/Minor Pentatonic Scales

___ C
- ___ 8ths
- ___ triplets
- ___ a minor pentatonic
- ___ patterns
- ___ all modes

___ Eb
- ___ 8ths
- ___ triplets
- ___ c minor pentatonic
- ___ patterns
- ___ all modes

___ Gb/F#
- ___ 8ths
- ___ triplets
- ___ eb minor pentatonic
- ___ patterns
- ___ all modes

___ A
- ___ 8ths
- ___ triplets
- ___ f# minor pentatonic
- ___ patterns
- ___ all modes

___ F
- ___ 8ths
- ___ triplets
- ___ d minor pentatonic
- ___ patterns
- ___ all modes

___ Ab
- ___ 8ths
- ___ triplets
- ___ f minor pentatonic
- ___ patterns
- ___ all modes

___ Cb/B
- ___ 8ths
- ___ triplets
- ___ ab minor pentatonic
- ___ patterns
- ___ all modes

___ D
- ___ 8ths
- ___ triplets
- ___ b minor pentatonic
- ___ patterns
- ___ all modes

___ Bb
- ___ 8ths
- ___ triplets
- ___ g minor pentatonic
- ___ patterns
- ___ all modes

___ Db/C#
- ___ 8ths
- ___ triplets
- ___ bb minor pentatonic
- ___ patterns
- ___ all modes

___ E
- ___ 8ths
- ___ triplets
- ___ c# minor pentatonic
- ___ patterns
- ___ all modes

___ G
- ___ 8ths
- ___ triplets
- ___ e minor pentatonic
- ___ patterns
- ___ all modes

Blues Scales

___ C
- ___ 8ths
- ___ triplets
- ___ 16ths
- ___ patterns
- ___ all modes

___ Eb
- ___ 8ths
- ___ triplets
- ___ 16ths
- ___ patterns
- ___ all modes

___ Gb/F#
- ___ 8ths
- ___ triplets
- ___ 16ths
- ___ patterns
- ___ all modes

___ A
- ___ 8ths
- ___ triplets
- ___ 16ths
- ___ patterns
- ___ all modes

___ F
- ___ 8ths
- ___ triplets
- ___ 16ths
- ___ patterns
- ___ all modes

___ Ab
- ___ 8ths
- ___ triplets
- ___ 16thspatterns
- ___ all modes

___ Cb/B
- ___ 8ths
- ___ triplets
- ___ 16ths
- ___ patterns
- ___ all modes

___ D
- ___ 8ths
- ___ triplets
- ___ 16ths
- ___ patterns
- ___ all modes

___ Db/C#
- ___ 8ths
- ___ triplets
- ___ 16ths
- ___ patterns
- ___ all modes

___ Bb
- ___ 8ths
- ___ triplets
- ___ 16ths
- ___ patterns
- ___ all modes

___ E
- ___ 8ths
- ___ triplets
- ___ 16ths
- ___ patterns
- ___ all modes

___ G
- ___ 8ths
- ___ triplets
- ___ 16ths
- ___ patterns
- ___ all modes

Find more Free resources at:

www.BasicJazzTheory.com

SCALE PRACTICE

There are very few human beings who receive the truth, complete and staggering,
by instant illumination. Most of them acquire it fragment by fragment, on a small
scale, by successive developments, cellularly, like a laborious mosaic.

~ Anaïs Nin

If music was genetic material, scales would be its DNA. Scales will give you a deeper understanding of melody and harmony, they will help your ear training, they will further your understanding of music theory, and they'll allow you to improvise and create melodies of your very own.

There are a lot of scales to learn and you may find it tough to keep track of where you are and where you need to go. Lucky for you, there is a solution. Just before these scales you saw a scale checklist. Post it in your practice room or leave it in your case. As you master certain scales and patterns, mark them off on the sheet. Once you've marked them all off, start over and get them faster. Scale practice is forever. The more you practice scales and all their patterns, the more fluid your playing will become.

GENERAL INFO ABOUT THESE SCALES

On the next few pages you'll find the major and natural minor scales, as well as major and minor pentatonics, and the blues scales. Sound like a lot of scales? There are many more, but these are the basics and will give you a good start. Start memorizing them now!

Remember that there are 15 major scales, but three of them overlap, so you'll really only be practicing the fingering for 12 scales. Confusing? You bet. If you remember enharmonic notes, you'll understand why this is. The Major Scales that overlap are D♭/C#, G♭/F#, and C♭/B. The minor scales that overlap are b♭/a#, e♭/d#, and a♭/g#. The fingerings and the sound of these enharmonic scales is the same, but they're written differently. It's like *to, too, two,* and *2.* They all sound the same but have different uses.

The scales are shown ascending only, but be sure to practice them going up, going down, and for as many octaves as you can comfortably play. Vary the speed, *start slowly,* and memorize them as soon as possible. Don't neglect the modes. Start on the second degree and go an octave for the Dorian mode. The third degree (Phrygian), fifth (Mixolydian), etc., etc. Apply the upcoming scale patterns to all the modes as well. You'll need to adapt the patterns for gapped scales or scales with less than 7 notes.

A Word on Memorization

Your goal with all of these scales is to memorize them. Memorize the scale, memorize the pattern, memorize the sound, memorize how it feels. When you memorize something it becomes part of you, it becomes internalized. All this memorization is like filling up a glass with clear water. As the glass becomes full, it will overflow. Stuff enough music into your brain and into your soul and soon it will overflow and you'll be making your own music, writing your own songs.

There is a Zen saying that goes, "The finger pointing at the moon is not the moon." It's the same with written music. Written music is only a guide. You are after the sound, not the note on the page. The sooner you memorize these scales and all the patterns, the more music you'll be able to create.

Once you have a scale's finger pattern memorized, you can practice the scale anywhere! As you practice the fingering away from the instrument, try to *hear* the notes and the intervals as you finger the scale. Try to visualize the scale too, if you can. This type of focused awareness is often more valuable than actual practice with the horn. Don't just sit there, finger you scales!

Scale Pattern Suggestions

Here are some ways to get these scales under your fingers. The numbers you see represent the degrees of the scale with 1 representing the tonic, or bottom note of the scale. Often at the beginning or end of the scale pattern, you'll go outside the octave. When you go below the tonic or root note, this is shown by a minus (-) sign. For example, one note below the tonic (the seventh degree of the scale) would be -7. In the key of C this would be the "B" just beneath the tonic. Going above the octave, just add another number. For example one note above the 8th note of the scale would be 9, then 10, etc. Here's what I mean.

These patterns may seem difficult to understand at first. To make these more clear, write out the number under each scale degree, then write out the scale pattern itself. Once you play these a few times, you'll hear the pattern and they will make more sense. Soon you'll be able to apply a pattern to a memorized scale without looking at the music. This is your goal.

Of course, these numbers only work with scales that have 8 notes, so for pentatonic and blues scale, you'll have to adapt your pattern for scales like these that have fewer notes. It's pretty easy once you have a pattern down with the major scale. Listen.

Pentatonics

Remember, to create a major pentatonic scale, you play the 1, 2, 3, 5, 6 degrees of the major scale. To play the minor pentatonic, use the 1, 3, 4, 5, 7 degrees of the natural minor scale. And the other reminder is that these will be the same notes for the relative minor/major scales. C Major pentatonic is C, D, E, G, A; the relative minor to C major (same notes, aka the Aeolian mode) is A natural minor, so the A minor pentatonic is A, C, D, E, G.

Pattern Name	Pattern
the scale	1,2,3,4,5,6,7,8,7,6,5,4,3,2,1
thirds	1,3,2,4,3,5,4,6,5,7,6,8,7,9,8,6,7,5,6,4,5,3,4,2,3,1,2,-7,1
fourths	1,4,2,5,3,6,4,7,5,8,6,9,7,10,8,5,7,4,6,3,5,2,4,1,3,-7,2,-6, 1
fifths	1,5,2,6,3,7,4,8,5,9,6,10,7,11,8,4,7,3,6,2,5,1,4,-7,3,-6,2,-5,1
rolling thirds	1,2,3,1,2,3,4,2,3,4,5,3,4,5,6,4,5,6,7,5,6,7,8,6,7,8,9,7,8 8,7,6,8,7,6,5,7,6,5,4,6,5,4,3,5,4,3,2,4,3,2,1,3,2,1,-7,2,1
rolling triplets (use 8th note triplet rhythm)	1,2,3,2,3,4,3,4,5,4,5,6,5,6,7,6,7,8,7,8,9,8 8,7,6,7,6,5,6,5,4,5,4,3,4,3,2,3,2,1,2,1,-7,1
rolling fifths	1,5,4,3,2,6,5,4,3,7,6,5,4,8,7,6,5,9,8,7,6,10,9,8,7,11,10,9,8 8,4,5,6,7,3,4,5,6,2,3,4,5,1,2,3,4,-7,1,2,3,-6,-7,1,2,-5,-6,-7,1
rolling fourths (use 8th note triplet rhythm)	1,4,3,2,5,4,3,6,5,4,7,6,5,8,7,6,9,8,7,10,9,8 8,5,6,7,4,5,6,3,4,5,2,3,4,1,2,3,-7,1,2,-6,-7,1

MAJOR SCALES

Flat Keys

Major Scales (flat keys continued)

Sharp Keys

Natural Minor Scales

Flat Keys

Natural Minor Scales

Sharp Keys

Blues Scales

Flat Keys

BLUES SCALES

Sharp Keys

A NOTE ON ENHARMONICS

Check out the D# and Eb blues scales. Play them both. Same fingerings and same sound, right? These are enharmonic scales, meaning they use different notes but have the same sound. This is one of those pesky facts of music theory that you simply don't run into if you play by ear. The only time you'll have to know the difference is if you're reading music and happen to be playing in D#, or some other weird enharmonic key. I can guarantee you that this is a RARE occurrence. In fact, in over 30 years of playing, I've never played a D# blues. Eb blues, yes, pretty often, but never in D#. Why bother when Eb is so much easier?

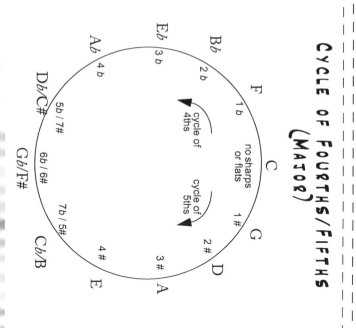

CYCLE OF FOURTHS/FIFTHS
(MAJOR)

cycle of 4ths

cycle of 5ths

C — no sharps or flats

F — 1 b
Bb — 2 b
Eb — 3 b
Ab — 4 b
Db/C# — 5b / 7#
Gb/F# — 6b / 6#
Cb/B — 7b / 5#
E — 4 #
A — 3 #
D — 2 #
G — 1 #

Chord Symbol	Meaning
min, -	minor
M, Ma, Maj, △	major
O	diminished
Ø	half-diminished
aug, +	augmented
7 (e.g. C^7)	add min 7 above chord root
9 (e.g. C^9)	add 9 above chord root (min 7 implied)
11 (e.g. C^{11})	add 11 above root (min7, 9 implied)
♯	raise 1/2 step
♭	lower 1/2 step

middle C is the C in the middle of your keyboard. Middle C as written in treble and bass clef looks like this:

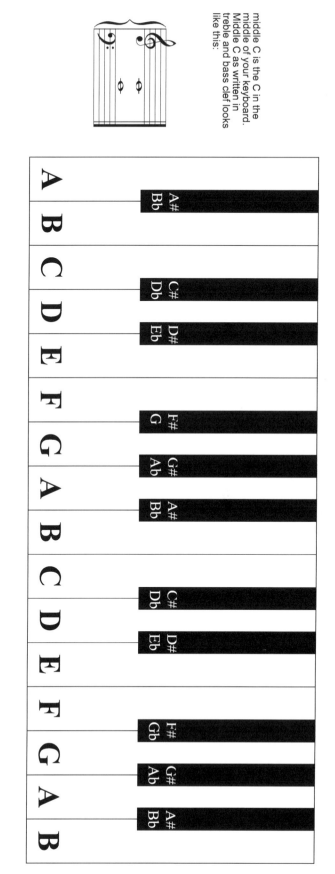

Guitar Fretboard

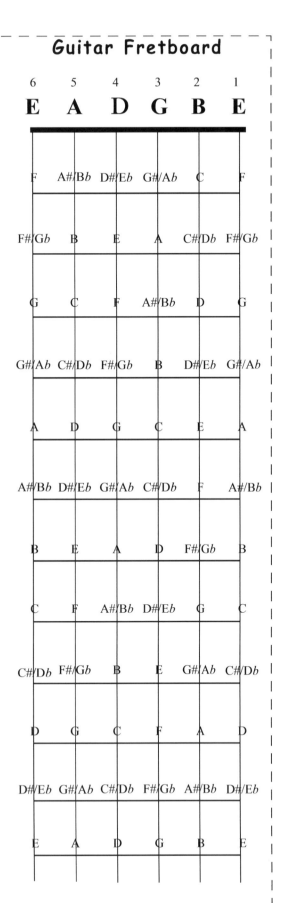

6	5	4	3	2	1
E	**A**	**D**	**G**	**B**	**E**

Chord Symbol	Meaning
min, –	minor
M, Ma, Maj, △	major
O	diminished
Ø	half-diminished
aug, +	augmented
7 (e.g. C^7)	add min 7 above chord root
9 (e.g. C^9)	add 9 above chord root (min 7 implied)
11 (e.g. C^{11})	add 11 above root (min7, 9 implied)
♯	raise 1/2 step
♭	lower 1/2 step

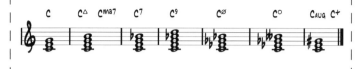

CYCLE OF FOURTHS/FIFTHS (NATURAL MINOR)

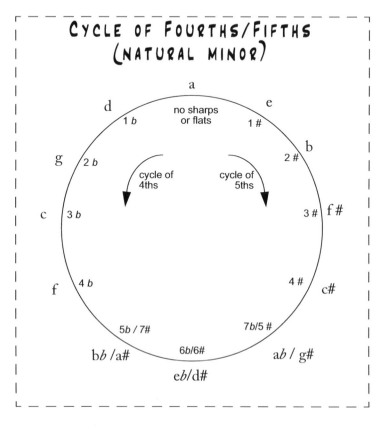

Made in the USA
Lexington, KY
27 July 2013